ROCKPEOPLE

ROCKPEOPLE

Ancient Man Captured in Stone

Michael G. Hunter

To order additional copies of this book, contact:
Xlibris
844-714-8691
www.Xlibris.com
Orders@Xlibris.com
832671

CONTENTS

ACKNOWLEDGMENTS

Chonosuke Okamura, a Japanese amateur paleontologist, discovered tiny people in rocks in limestone from Nagiawa, Japan (Northeast Japan, Honshu Island). The Okamura Fossil Laboratory documented his findings in several books published in the 1980s. He documented the people and animals he saw as microscopic, measuring 3.5 millimeters in size, and he believed they lived during the Silurian age, about 400 million years ago. His work was the instigation and inspiration for this book.

Chonosuke Okamura's books, with photos in black and white, taken through microscope, called the people he saw "minipeople," "minimen," "minimankind," or "mini homo," giving them scientific names, as a subspecies of *Homo sapiens*, which he called "*Homo sapiens minilorientales*." In his books, he describes what he saw in high level of detail, showing that the minimen wore buttoned clothing, had hair styles, and were surrounded by other types of tiny creatures (dogs, dragons, etc.), for which he also assigned scientific names. He recorded over eighty species of animals, including dinosaurs.

I would thank Chonosuke Okamura, if he were alive. Even his foundation, the Okamura Fossil Laboratory, no longer exists, most likely dying with him. Therefore, I extend blessings to his spirit and his discoveries.

Another writer has had strong influence on my studies, and credit is due to him: Immanuel Velikovsky, the Russian who, like Okamura, is frowned upon by science, yet he investigated in depth the possibility of collisions of planets, primarily from the perspective of ancient writings, myths, and legends. His controversial writings in *Worlds in Collision*, *Ages in Chaos*, and *Earth in Upheaval* gave me a crucial understanding of how worlds might have collided in the distant, forgotten past, leaving mysterious effects on the Earth.

Physicist Richard Muller was another important influence on my studies as his book *Nemesis* gave me the clue to the cause of world collisions (sunpartners). He gave me permission to publish his extinction charts in my books on Mars, in which I give still another perspective on the subject of world collisions and possibility of one or more sunpartners that influence our planet.

A local paleontologist, Ken Finger, helped date the rocks in Niles Canyon area as in the Knoxville formation, which dates to Cretaceous, 66–145 million years ago, uplifted by the Hayward fault. This probably means, and I interpret it so, that rocks from an earlier age were brought to the surface by seismic activity during that period.

The Institute of Human Origins at Arizona State University disappointedly deems this subject "outside of their realm of study" and was, therefore, not interested.

The Berkeley Geochronology Center, which dates rocks using argon, was unable to support my request for dating of samples because they were too busy.

INTRODUCTION

There have been times when our wondrous planet Earth was covered with people, not just people as we know them today but people of all different sizes who were flash-frozen and then petrified, becoming stone. In spite of great significance to our understandings of the origin of mankind, scientists (paleontologists, anthropologists, archaeologists, astrobiologists, and others) generally prefer to ignore the phenomenon because it seemingly does not fit with modern evolutionary theory and leads to confusion about current beliefs. And so the subject has been essentially unexplored.

In the 1970s and 1980s, a Japanese amateur paleontologist, Chonosuke Okamura, delved into the subject, documenting his observations. After extensive examination of rocks from a mountain in Japan, he concluded that they contained miniscule people. What I have seen is far more extensive than Okamura's minimen in several ways. The size of the people in rocks that I have observed varies considerably, from microscopic, even smaller than those Okamura described, to as well as much larger, even larger than ourselves. Also, they occur in many types of rocks. And still further, they occur in rocks of many ages, throughout the billions of years that Earth has existed. In examining a variety of types of rocks from many sources, I have found not only people, but also animals, including dinosaur-looking creatures, although my primary interest in writing this book is in the humanlike creatures.

The rockpeople extent, as I observed, was vast, throughout this planet, as I have seen them in rocks from Canada, Great Britain, Japan, North and South America, and elsewhere around the globe. The rockpeople seemingly covered the Earth during the time or times they thrived. Unlike primitive man as we now theorize him, the rockpeople can be seen to have lived in a highly-developed society, not unlike our own, with clothing, hats, sunglasses, houses, and metal devices, such as telescopes and even vehicles. They seem much like ourselves, physically and behaviorally, although we Earthlings have probably surpassed them technologically in recent times, with our large-scale transportation, space, and electronics industries, as well as science. There is no evidence, to my awareness, of ancient roadways, railroad tracks, or industrial complexes, although those things cannot be ruled out because I have seen just a trifel of what actually existed in their time. The animals that I have observed are of various sorts and sizes, not just minicreatures, but larger ones.

The images in rocks that I present in this book are, unfortunately, for several reasons, difficult to see. Since those who cannot see the images may simply not understand or appreciate what is in this book and may consider them doubtful, improbable, or unlikely, without due cause or consideration, I recommend taking a second and longer look at each image, spending more time than normal, to allow your eyes and mind to study and understand them. I have tried to limit the images to those most visible, although I do understand that some people will be unable to "see" them.

This subject, I gather from discussions with others and with the science community's response to Chonosuke Okamura, is considered "pseudoscience," generally ignored and disbelieved, like other subjects of my interest, such as life on Mars or on the Moon. In my publications (*Life on Mars*, 2012; *Life on Mars 2*, 2013; and *Life on Mars 3*, 2014), I analyzed Mars rover photos carefully and drew conclusions from my observations. From those first publications, I have determined that there are two essential problems with the subject: (1) people have been led to believe that life does not exist on other worlds brought about by scientific reports, teachings, and studies; and (2) people have difficulty in "seeing" images, such as rover photos, because of poor photo quality. Hence, careless examination brings up a sort of mental block, or refusal to accept, as it conflicts harshly with known and scientific theories and beliefs. Very few people on Earth consider it feasible that there is life on Mars or on the Earth's Moon or on other planets. Believing in such things is similar to, and as difficult as, trying to convert a person's religion or political party. People, not only scientists, do not accept change of their longstanding beliefs easily. People generally trust science, even as it filters down to the public through the education and information system.

———

I have tried, without success, to enlist support from several people. Famed forensic geologist Scott Wolters seemed barely interested. Local paleontologist Ken Finger considered the images "coincidences of nature." Relatives, friends, and neighbors listen to me for short periods in patient disbelief but then often seem to act as if I must have lost my reason without trying to explore the subject on their own. The response of people in the Human Origins Association in Berkeley, California, is it does not consider it "within their realm of study." The people in the Geochronology Center in Berkeley were "too busy" to date a few rocks for me. In fact, Chonosude Okamura, a bona fide scientist (amateur paleontologist), had similar difficult experiences in convincing others of his findings. That people can be seen in rocks seems to everyone else to be something impossible and likely unreal or delusionary. In spite of my own bad experiences in finding support, however, I do see encouragement in that scientists do actually claim to search for extraterrestrial life with passionate zeal, and anthropologists argue even today about the beginnings of mankind from their observations, regardless of the scarcity of and poor quality of fossils and sometimes the questionability of their dating. Human origins are continuously being updated.

It occurs to me that subjects such as this will be not given any significant importance for many years to come, perhaps for decades or even centuries in the future, long after I am gone. I take encouragement from the fact that Isaac Newton's writings about laws of motion and universal gravitation were essentially ignored for two centuries, long after he died, and yet today they have become, to some extent, common knowledge, even taught now in public education. Also, we have progressed somewhat since the time when Galileo was punished as a heretic for his astronomical studies of other planets with a crude telescope. Copernicus, for his studies of the solar system organization, with his studies showing that the Earth was not the center of the solar system, similarly, was somewhat unrecognized, disbelieved, and ignored for centuries, yet today he is recognized as one of the first to realize the simple truth that the Sun does not orbit the Earth. And so seeing how people are slow to accept some truths, and yet they finally blossomed, however gradually, I do have small hopes that in the distant future, possibly centuries from now, learned people will someday come to a point where they investigate and understand their prehistoric past much better than they do now. I have come to accept that people are simply not ready for the information in this book.

———

My primary explanation of the existence of *Homo sapiens* on Mars, presented in my second and third books about life on Mars, is my theory that the two planets, Mars and Earth, came together at the time of the Great Deluge, or Noah, 4,800 years ago, and very likely, every 37.5 million years, on a regular basis (based on dinosaurs on Mars that are now extinct on Earth). That theory explained a lot of the Martian cultural appearances, clothing styles, and a lot of the archaeological artifacts that seem to have come from a particular swath of Earth's populated area at the time.

The public does not question science at this time in mankind's development, similar to the way science was once considered an assault on religion five hundred years ago. Evidence to support my conclusions is sparse: fuzzy photos that most people seem to be unable to interpret, deductive reasoning that contradicts scientific theories such as evolution, absence of life on other planets or on the Moon, the Great Deluge. I have listed what supporting evidence I can in my books, but of course, it is not "proven," just my own theory. It seems hardly worth the effort to study (to scientists) because there seems so little real material to actually study (other than in the lithifications that cover the Earth). The primary evidence for life on Mars, as I see it, is in Mars rover photos, but that, of course, is not of a quality that allows any kind of credibility from scientists. Secondary evidence includes references in ancient writings, myths, and legends, such as the stories of Noah and his ark and the "fallen ones" or Nephilim. Those are vague, controversial, distant, and as if by collective amnesia, easily regarded by science as no more than handed-down myths or legends, barely evidence, not even close to proven scientific facts. Some of that type of myths or legends were recalled and considered in books like *Worlds in Collision* and *Earth in Upheaval* by Immanuel Velikovsky, while scientists don't particularly care much about that somewhat scattered and unscientific type of presentation. UFOs and Bigfoot sightings are regarded similarly. The difficulties in visually interpreting the massively-available evidence makes any theory questionable in nature or perhaps unproven and, therefore, not worthy of consideration. If Earth and Mars did scrape, then there should be some evidence of that, such as Mars-origin rocks or soil in the location of contact, as well as Earth-origin material on Mars. However, that would mean evidence of the scrape on Earth is probably inaccessible, at the bottom of the oceans or the Mediterranean Sea, possibly, most likely, and traces of Earth on Mars. To find it and recognize it would be quite difficult, something like finding a needle in a haystack. It could be buried under Earth's soil or rocks. Five thousand years is a significant length of time for it to become intermixed caused by tides, waves, erosion, plant growth, weather, or earthquakes. So the easiest and most likely way to study the question lies on Mars itself and in man's exploration of that planet, which is, unfortunately, five years or more in the future at this time. Scientists today seem blind to life outside of the Earth; and therefore, to them, there is none. It will, unfortunately, take time, lots of time, for a gradual scientific revolution to occur in that regard. Therefore, this book is somewhat unlikely to become accepted and not going to rock any boats or cause any kind of action or reaction anywhere, leaving a somewhat disappointing, frustrating, and disgusting situation, which was not unlike the experiences of Copernicus, Galileo, Newton, and others. Hence, these types of studies are "beyond science."

One would think that the photos from NASA's rovers, satellites, and probe show the truth. Photos don't lie; seeing is believing. But the photos achieved thus far, at this time, are not doing much in terms of showing the truth. People have remarked to me that I am seeing things like they see images in clouds or popcorn ceilings or in their marble shower walls. The photos are, in a nutshell, to most people who look at them, "blurry pictures," nothing more. I agree that scientists generally cannot make judgments based on blurry photographs that don't make sense to them. And most people cannot extend their vision to "fill the blanks" or to "connect the dots." On top of looking blurry, as if one were looking through frosted glass or fog, the colors are bleached as if not developed thoroughly. And then to make things totally on the verge of uselessness, they are "still" photographs, not movies, and rarely do we see a second shot of the same thing to indicate movement. So the photos, rover photos, rockpeople photos, are, basically, showing what the typical skeptical scientist interprets as a barren, dry desert on Mars and rocky accumulations on smaller bodies with no evidence of life whatsoever. The living animals and people are, however, easily visible, when the photos are enhanced with enlargement, higher contrast, higher color saturation, and lower light levels. Knowing now about those problems, I have done the best I can in this book to limit and enhance the photos to the point where I believe others can or at least, might see them. And so the new daily photos from Mars, full of living beings and their livelihood, are of such poor quality as to never be seen clearly without great effort. Occasional pictures are examined by those with good eyes and open minds, but for the most part, the photos become easily forgotten and passed by, dropped into files that nobody ever studies. And so a planet full of living beings is not even considered as a source of life other than possibly microbial.

These things require an open mind. Perhaps open-mindedness is something that is very rare throughout the history of mankind, by few people and during few occasions. I believe, however, that it does occur as I have experienced it myself to some degree; and I believe very strongly that it can be, has been, and will be experienced by others. The open mind is at least partially a result of eliminating blockages. We seem to have blockages in our mind, which are created as learning experiences, such as the foods we eat. As schoolchildren, we "learn" that life is impossible on Mars and the Moon, for example. Thus, we take it for granted, that nothing is living there and don't pursue. An analogy would be similar to worm-eating; those who grew up eating worms eat them with enjoyment and for nourishment, while those who grew up without them eat them only with fear and disgust. The blockage exists in the non-worm-eater, yet it can be removed with effort. Someone visiting a worm-eater, for example, might be put into the awkward position of having to eat one out of social courtesy. In that case, if the person does actually eat a worm, then he may do so but still find the taste and texture unacceptable. To remove the blockage, one needs to be in a situation of repeatedly eating worms, out of necessity perhaps, and developing a taste for them. So it is with the exploration/finding of life on Mars or on the Moon. One has to first "find" a life-form, as I found a sand dollar in rover photos, and then with optimism and unblocked vision, search for more, find them, and then attempt to share the information with a book such as this.

There are conspiracy theorists that say NASA and "the government" are all treating us like idiots, hiding the facts about extraterrestrial life, feeding us disinformation, because they have a secret agenda of domination that cannot be avoided. Another similar theory is that they are afraid we will all panic if we knew the truth. But I disagree with those theories. I don't think so. Scientists, from what I see, are simply blind about life on Mars, and attempts to break through their walls are as likely to convince them as blind men describing an elephant from their sense of touch; "the blind are leading the blind." And so extraterrestrial life on the Moon or on Mars or on other planets is ignored and disbelieved.

Most people on Earth are not ready for life outside of their home planet, primarily because of the misperception/fallacy that has been created and supported by science's conspiracy of silence and by astronomers and by astrobiologists over the past several decades. My first three books, each of them, came as a surprise, even to me, as I continued to be astounded and amazed the more I looked at the photos. I really thought I was finished when I finished each book. But then time passed, and I found more to document. Since publishing the book *Life on Mars 3* in early 2014, I have since found cars, gold coins, beer or water or soda cans, micropeople, and other discoveries in Mars rover photos that gradually brought me to the point where I feel a need to do more documentation of my astounding findings, regardless of whether people can see or believe me.

1

Method

My method of study for this book on rockpeople includes taking photographs of rocks, which I then view and enlarge on a large computer screen. In some cases, such as Moon rocks, asteroids, online images of meteorites or Google Earth photos, I did not personally take the photographs; I simply enlarged them for observation and documentation purposes. To avoid copyright issues, I am including only my own photos except that NASA photos of Moonpeople is allowable to NASA. In addition to the photographic step, there are other steps involved in the process: memory and logic. Memory is necessary to reveal patterns. For example, observation of sunglasses, face masks, or telescopes in multiple images leads to the conclusion that the rockpeople commonly used those articles. Logic is necessary to derive the conclusion that there was some sort of mass-production process involved in making their sunglasses and telescopes, and therefore, by observing a multitude of rock images, and with applied logic and memory, the conclusion can be derived that the rockpeople were able to design and manufacture objects made with glass and metal, much as we do today with industrialized production. So mankind has reinvented necessary objects over many periods, not necessarily for the first time in our understanding.

The scientific method supported by modern scientists and applicable to their work in modern times has a clear methodology in deriving conclusions from observations. In developing a general theory, in using the pure scientific method, the new theory must be consistent with other current theories. This is one of the greatest problems I face in this subject.

My findings, at first glance, are totally inconsistent with other current theories (for example, evolution) and are, therefore, unacceptable to modern scientists. However, it is my contention that what I am observing is not contradictory, but rather complementary, to existing theories.

Chonosuke Okamura made errors in his conclusions because of his limited method (photography through microscope) and limited sample size (his local area of Japan), so I realize it is possible that my own conclusions are to some degree erroneous in spite of my larger sample size, using things other than a microscope (computer), looking at other solar system bodies, using rover photos and telescopic astrophotos, *Apollo* astronaut photos on the Moon, photos from the Internet, and my own camera photos. He did not see that there are rockpeople of various sizes. This suggests that he may have presumed that he could only see them with a microscope; whereas, on the contrary, I have found that the larger people are quite visible with the naked eye and even from aerial photos. He named them "*Homo sapiens miniorientalis,*" thinking they only occurred in miniature size (mini) and only in the oriental zone on Earth (*orientalis*). Thus, he likely presumed only on the basis of what he saw and did not extend through logic that they occurred in various sizes and worldwide. Or it might be that, in loyalty to true scientific method, he could not use as evidence that which he could not observe. In other words, he was hampered by his tools and by his own "scientific method."

The obvious contradiction between my conclusions and known scientific theories of evolution and origin of mankind will no doubt lead to controversy, if not outright opposition. Nevertheless, as far as I can tell, my observations did lead me to my conclusions, and as old sayings go, "Seeing is believing," and "What you see is what you get," regardless of whether it is consistent with current theories, which may or may not be true.

I have observed rocks from various places and supposedly from different ages. Granite river rocks, worn to oval shapes from water, from California's hills in the East Bay, are estimated to be no more than 200 million years old. In fact, geology books state that there are no rocks in the East Bay older than 200 million years. The Japanese limestone that Chonosoke Okamura studied was estimated by him to be from Silurian age, i.e., 400 million years old. The rocks brought back by astronauts from the Moon are considered over 4 billion years old. The red lava rocks I have studied from Sibley Volcanic Reserve in Berkeley are likely from the latest eruption, only 10 million years ago. Similarly, Lassen rocks are likely to be no more than 30 million years old, when volcanic activity began in that region. And rocks on the volcanic Hawaiian island of Oahu are likely to be only 3 million years old. Yet I have observed petrified people in all those.

Real or Imaginary

No doubt, many people will judge, prematurely, that the images of minipeople, as presented by Chonosuke Okamura, as well as my own presentation herein, are not real but simply a product of my imagination. The images are not totally clear, not totally obvious. The presence of humans in 400 million-year-old rocks flies contrary to beliefs of modern science, that humankind evolved from apes only 5 million years ago, and cannot be considered "believable" to most people for the sake of "science" alone. The rockpeoples' existence contradicts our understanding, our intelligence, our logic. On top of that, the scientific understanding of the concept of pareidolia suggests that it is a possible cause of the conundrum. So the question is, how can we distinguish between pareidolia and real? The answer—in several ways: shape, level of detail, multiplicity, color, and shadow. The explanation to the question is that the more complex an image appears, the more likely it is real. We need to pursue far beyond a first-impression inkblot test.

Shape

The shape of an image can be the first indicator of what it truly is. A human head is a very recognizable shape: two eyes, one mouth, one nose, two ears, head and facial hair, etc. We learn instinctively as babies to recognize and even distinguish other people by their faces. Mother, father, and other family members and relatives have unique appearances relating to size and shape. Pareidolia effect in each of us suggests that we see human faces where there are none, such as in cheese sandwiches or even the age-old "man in the Moon." So the common occurrence of eyelike objects above a nose and mouth, with ears, is apparent everywhere and should be considered simply figments of our minds' imaginations. Surely, before we consider this type of anomaly "real," we need to examine it further. We need to scrutinize beyond first impression.

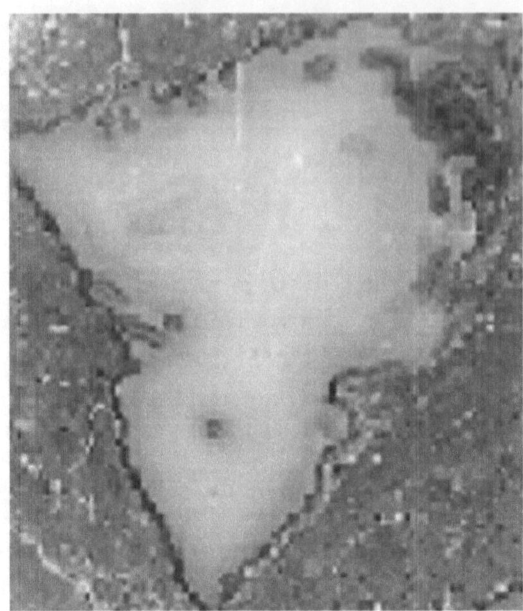

PAREIDOLIA FACE IMAGE IN CUT/POLISHED MEXICAN GEODE

Level of Detail

A cloud can form to resemble something: a fish, a human, anything. However, the cloud is a constantly-changing shape, and usually, if we watch it, we can see it change from a recognizable form to a meaningless shape over time. People have a unique capability to see meaningful shapes in places that they are obviously not what they appear: Jesus in a cheese sandwich, Our Lady of Guadalupe in a mark on a tree. But such images are just vague, lacking in detail, monotone, and clearly likely to be imaginary and coincidental. However, if you see a cloud shaped like a human wearing a pair of sunglasses or a brown derby hat or standing next to a woman with a red dress, then you are more probably not watching a cloud but something real.

The amount of detail in a pareidolic image is limited. For example, in a cloud formation, the general shape of a head might occur by coincidence, with several features, such as a neck, a chin, eyes, a nose, and a mouth. However, beyond that, it would be highly unlikely for the head to have a colored hat or to be wearing dark glasses or to have more detailed features, such as hair style, clothing style, and other such detail. Therefore, when an image becomes detailed beyond a certain degree, it can be judged to be a real object rather than an illusion. It helps to count the features of an image that looks humanlike, such as body shape, head shape, eyes, nose, mouth, beard, ears, arms, legs, shirt, pants, belt, etc. An item with twelve features is more likely real than an item with three.

Multiplicity

Sometimes a cloud formation breaks into several similar formations, such as two or more fish. But they are obviously not fish; they are constantly changing shape and lacking in eyes, mouth, and fins. A group of similar objects is one way to assess whether it is real or imaginary. Several similar objects suggest more real than not, although, of course, it is not conclusive without other indications, such as color or other detailed features. I have seen two clouds that look like two similar fish, but of course, they eventually dissipated and, therefore, were not real fish. But ten fishlike clouds (or fossils) would be more likely real than one or two. So multiple objects give us clues to the objects' reality but not proof.

Color

Color is a great help in determining whether an image is real or imaginary. If there is no color, an image is more likely to be imaginary. But when colors appear in the appropriate places, that is a clue that the image is real. For example, flesh tones on a face, hair color on top of the head, red lips, and clothing colors, likewise, boost the acknowledgment of real versus imagined.

Shadow

People who have been petrified in rocks do not have shadows. This is a logical phenomenon, coming from the assumption that shadows cannot be included in the petrification process. The process includes a molecular displacement of material, and a shadow, of course, is not a material but rather a visual effect from absence of light. Therefore, in petrification, people, their clothing, their features, such as hair and skin color, and their material effects in general, are preserved, yet they do not have shadows. The dark spots that we see on their eyes, for example, is often simply dark glasses that they are wearing over their eyes. The absence of shadow does give us a clue that it is not simply a photographic image.

All the Above

Consider the question of real or imaginary using the four concepts above on the following image taken from a rock. There are two humanoid-shaped figures recognizable as a man and woman, with heads, eyes, hair, and clothing. The man has a red hat or cap. The woman has long blond hair. The man is dressed in black, while he woman is in white. They appear to be wearing dark glasses and face masks as well as headdresses. Overall, it appears much like a wedding picture. It is difficult to imagine that all this detail is simply coincidental or imaginary. Therefore, it most likely is a real representation of what is described.

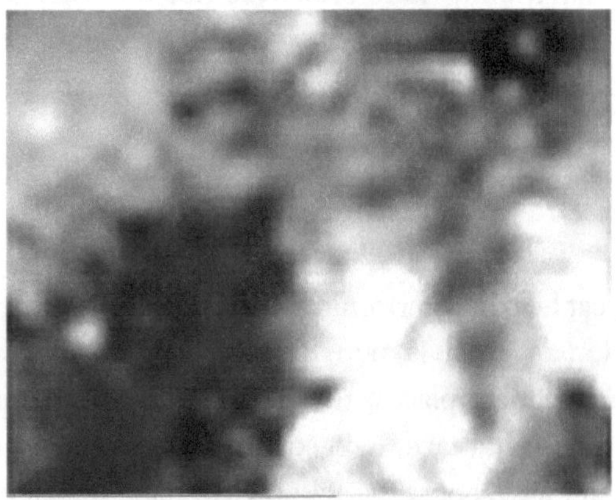

WEDDING GROOM AND BRIDE, FREMONT, CALIFORNIA

Real or Just Images

Similar to the question of whether the minipeople are real or imaginary, there is another question: Are they real objects, or are they simply images, like photographs? This has to do with dimensions. Real objects are generally three-dimensional, whereas images are two-dimensional. This can be observed in clear rocks like crystals. If an image is two-dimensional, one could look at it from many angles and determine that. But if it is three-dimensional, that would also be obvious in a clear medium. Shadow also is part of the image of real things, and so if there are shadows, then more likely it is not just an image but a real entity. In absence of shadows, it is not real but a representation. So what the minipeople are is not real, not images, but representations. They are real representations real representations (petrifications).

Edge Wrap

This question, two- or three-dimensional, can be evaluated on an opaque specimen by looking at the object in detail. For example, on a rounded river rock, does an object seem to wrap around the curvature of the rock, or does it appear to be cut away where the rock was eroded by action in the river? A two-dimensional object would not wrap around a worn edge.

Embedment

If an object is three-dimensional, then only a portion of it will be visible in a rock as the depth of the object becomes embedded in the rock, just as a person or animal that floats in water has only a small portion above the surface. This explains why it is that with many of the rockpeople, the only visible part is the head. However, just as we see someone's body floating in transparent water, we see the entire body in transparent silica, such as crystal.

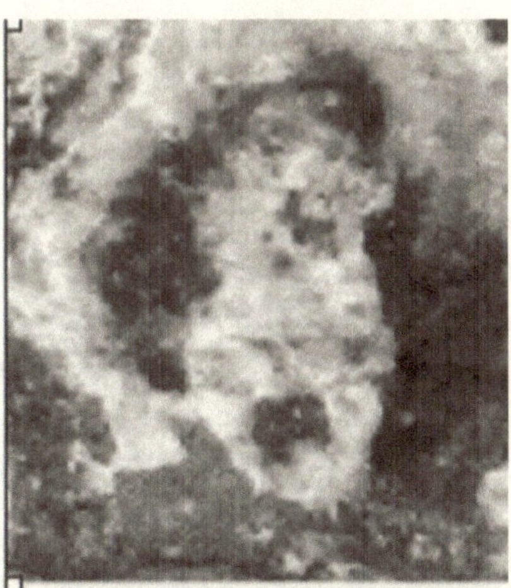

MINIWOMAN SCREAMING, FREMONT, CALIFORNIA

2

Related Studies

It is generally presumed, putting biblical theory aside, that mankind evolved from an inferior species over the past several million years. Contradictory arguments against evolutionary theory are sparse and baseless. Scientific findings, comparisons, and developments, such as carbon dating and DNA analysis, have supported strong beliefs about the early beginnings of *Homo sapiens* as *Cro-Magnon* roughly three hundred thousand years ago in Northern Africa.

In the 1970s and 1980s, the Japanese paleontologist Chonosuke Okamura concluded from his observations of rocks that there were miniature people on Earth that became embedded in 400 million-year-old Japanese limestone in what we call the Silurian period. He found tiny animals also and gave what he saw scientific names, such as "*Homo sapiens mini*" and "*Canis mini*" (dog). Unfortunately, his findings, as important as they might be for modern understanding of human origin, are essentially ignored and forgotten by science, for they frustratingly contradict modern beliefs and understandings to an extent deemed unacceptable. It defies logic, for most, that humankind, who evolved only during the recent past few million years, can be seen in rocks that are hundreds of millions of years old. This conundrum can be seen in a couple of examples of Okamura's finding. His work is considered pareidolia or pseudoscience, unacceptable to mainstream scientific understandings or beliefs.

Curious about this subject, in late 2015, I tracked down Okamura's books at the University of California Paleontology Library and studied his photographs. I agreed with his observations and felt that they were quite reasonable, with the exception that he did not seem to realize that there were various sizes of people. After all, his tools for observing were probably limited to microscopes and magnifying glasses, without the magnificent improvements available today in computers and digital photography with capabilities such as contrast and color enhancement as well as unlimited magnification. Also, he published his images in black and white only, which, of course, allows only a partial presentation. A few of his photos can be found online.

Petradox and Coso Artifact

Upon pursuing the subject further, I began to look at mystifying stones, such as the Petradox (also called the Enigmalith) found in 1998 on a hike in an undisclosed location by John J. Williams, who lives in New Mexico, and the Coso Artifact found in California in 1961; both of which seem to have embedment of modern-day electrical objects in age-old granite or sandstone. Although both are generally considered to be hoaxes, I analyzed the stones in which they are embedded for minicreatures simply by enlargement of available photos online.

My reasoning was that if the modern electronic items had become embedded in the rocks fairly recently, perhaps the rocks are simply concrete that had been mixed and poured, and the objects in them were manufactured in modern times and aged rapidly. In that case, no minipeople or minicreatures would be evident in them. But to my amazement, on close examination of online photos, I saw that the rocks had tiny humanoid-looking creatures in them, similar to those found by Okamura in his limestone, and therefore, I concluded they were, in fact, ancient stones, not modern concrete. The Enigmalith has been dated at one hundred thousand years old. Whether the embedded item in it is the same age as the stone, I leave to others to decide. As for the Coso Artifact, it is much like a 1920s spark plug imbedded in a five-hundred-thousand-year-old geode. It appears entirely possible that ancient peoples had the technological capability suggested by the artifacts. My own conclusion is that these stones are ancient, and they contain images of ancient creatures and are not manufactured hoaxes.

My studies then progressed beyond stones of interest on the Internet to observe stones that I had near my home and that I had accumulated over time and kept for sentimental reasons. In the 1990s, my parents had a lapidary business in which they cut geodes in half, polished them, and then sold them in arts and crafts fairs. In fact, I also had and accumulated a collection of various semiprecious rocks, such as agates, jade, turquoise, lapis lazuli, and others over time. Another source was stones that I had found on daily walks and in travels. But after looking at my collection of rocks and seeing the minipeople in virtually every stone from around the world (on the Internet), I have to conclude that there *are* such people, locked into nearly every stone throughout the planet. There may be exceptions, as my samples are of limited quantity and from limited locations, but until now, I have not found them. I did find a pebble in Watsonville, California, that contained only fish. Perhaps pure precious stones like diamonds and rubies are exceptions? That is a question yet unresolved.

Although it seems contrary to everything modern scientists know about the evolution of mankind, Okamura came to his conclusions because the formation of igneous stone in Japan where he studied was generally of Silurian age as he determined, I imagine, by scientific geologic theory and methods. Although the petrification or silification process can occur in a minimum of fifty thousand years, making the effect possible within the time span of known *Homo sapiens*, formation of igneous rocks worldwide cannot have been in such short periods. My studies and findings are somewhat diverse, and I have tried to age-date rocks using fairly simplistic reasoning, without the ability of such methods unavailable to me as radioactive decay. The most recently formed stones that I have examined thus far would be those of Hawaii, in the island of Oahu, which, geologists claim, were formed as islands during volcanic eruption about 1–3 million years ago. The stones in the area where I live, in the San Francisco East Bay Area, according to geologic study, rose from lower depths or were formed because of seismic activity around 200 million years ago at the earliest. Also, the stones of the Mount Lassen area appear to be more recent, and geologic publications suggest that the lava flowed from that source within the past few million years. The oldest stones I have examined, through photographs on the Internet, range more than 4 billion years, such as the oldest known rocks on Earth, Internet photos of meteorites, some dated 2 billion years old, and rocks brought back from the Moon by astronauts, which date older than the Earth. The sizes of people in my findings, unlike Okamura's, are quite various, from microscopic beings to giants bigger than normal people on Earth today.

The Nampa Figure

Lending credence to the contradiction against evolutionary theory is the Nampa Figurine, a clay figure unearthed from 300 feet below the surface of the ground in Nampa, Idaho, in 1889. The clay figure is without doubt from an era estimated to be 2 million years ago. The figurine, anatomically the same as *Homo sapiens*, wears clothing and jewelry that could pass us on the street unnoticed today. At 2 million years old, it preceded any early human predecessor.

Interplanetary Exchanges

In my first book, *Life on Mars*, my observations of many animals like Earth's on Mars led me to question, how could it be possible that the same animals, which have existed on Earth for only the past tens of thousands of years, also exist on Mars? There are not a lot of plausible explanations: (1) the animals evolved at the same time on both planets; (2) the animals somehow were transported from one planet to another. The probability of evolution on both planets at the same time seems highly unlikely as the environments are so different. Mars's atmosphere, for example, has a tiny fraction of the oxygen as on Earth. Water is much more available on Earth. The Earth went through extinctions of animals, such as the dinosaurs, yet Mars did not (examples of dinosaurs, such as brontosaurus, stegosaurus, and pterodactyl, were observed in my books *Life on Mars*). The current *Homo sapiens* species, in fact, evolved, as far as scientists know, in the past three hundred thousand years as fossils of the species have not been found older than that. The environments on the two planets are so different; the idea that the same animals evolved in different environments seems ludicrous. That reasoning led me to the conclusion that there had to have been a transfer, an exchange, between planets.

So if one concludes that there was an "exchange" of life-forms from Earth to Mars and possibly the other direction, it leads to the further conclusion that the two planets collided in the past. Other evidence that supports the theory of interplanetary exchanges includes the extinction chart, from the book *Nemesis* by Richard Muller, which shows periodic massive extinctions over time. Still more evidence can be found in the ancient and worldwide legendary story of Noah's ark, which was found with 99.9 percent certainty, (admittedly, with obvious scientific skepticism), at elevation of 12,000 feet above sea level on Mount Ararat; how could water level have risen to over 2 miles above sea level without some huge gravitational attraction such as a passing planet like Mars?

My study of the periodicity of extinction events, combined with my observations of animal types on Mars, led me to propose that the Earth and Mars collided periodically because of the influence of sunpartners and, in fact, at the time of the Great Deluge, around five thousand years ago. That is all detailed in my second book *Life on Mars 2* and further clarified in the third, *Life on Mars 3*. The conclusion that I reached from that study was that planets collided because of sunpartner influence and, more specifically, the differential ellipticalization of their orbits. In other words, the slower speeds of outer planets lead to greater ellipticallization of orbits than the faster inner planets, thereby causing an overlap of orbits and potential collisions. The concept is similar to the way bullets fired horizontally at differing muzzle velocities will travel different distances.

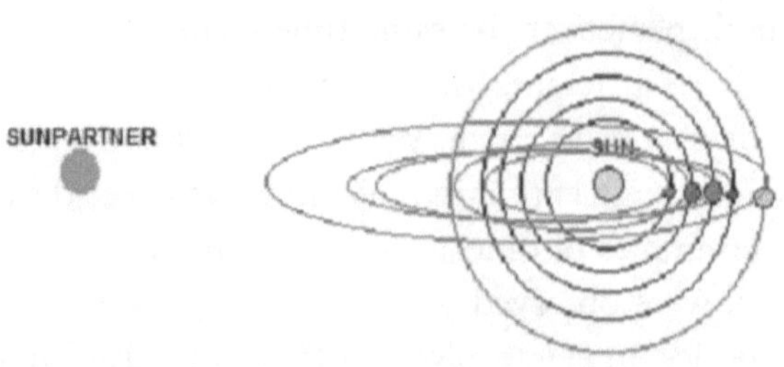

ELLIPTICAL ORBITS CAUSED BY SUNPARTNER

This concept is vital in understanding the cause of rockpeople, as the only plausible explanation I can imagine for people becoming frozen instantly, in the blink of an eye, is with some kind of instantaneous super-low temperature such as in the atmosphere of Jupiter, which is now known to be roughly 300 degrees below zero.

One thing I have yet to address is the sunpartner effect on the Earth's Moon. Obviously, the Moon's orbit around Earth would similarly turn elongated during the approach of the sunpartner. But furthermore, during a brush with another planet, such as Mars or Jupiter, the Moon orbit would be pulled elliptically toward the planet it orbits. During the brush with Mars, which is what I have concluded is what occurred during Noah's flood, it was coincidental that the Moon did not collide with Mars. Perhaps it was simply that the likelihood of the Moon plunging directly into Mars is quite improbable, considering that the Moon's orbit is 360 degrees, while the window of collision with Mars while it passed within the orbit might have been only on the order of 10 degrees or even less. Also, the Moon's orbit inclination might have further reduced the probability. But with Jupiter brushing the Earth, it is much more likely that the Earth's Moon passed through Jupiter's atmosphere, along with Earth, freezing its surface.

Although the Moon, during a planetary approach, may not have literally "collided" with Earth, the gravitational effects on the great water body on Earth might have "washed" things from Earth to Moon, as well as in the other direction.

It seems possible that the Earth passed only partially within Jupiter's atmosphere, or similarly, all life on Earth did not freeze. This is evident in the considerations that (1) humans, dogs, cats, birds, elephants, hippos, rhinoceros, and many other animals, thought of today as of African origin, have apparently survived on Earth and still can be seen on Earth's Moon, in Earth rocks, and living today, apparently throughout the 400-million-year period since the brush; (2) the African continent is considered the cradle or origin of mankind during the recent late Pleistocene era; (3) the seven continents as we know them today are not configured the same as they were hundreds of millions of years ago; they were all together in a single supercontinent, Pangea; (4) the poles of Earth may have changed as result of or since the brush; (5) the great freeze or pass through Jupiter's atmosphere might not have affected animals that were burrowed deeply underground or deep in the ocean because of the warmth of Earth's core and the insulation value of the soil, while the duration may have been short. Therefore, one side of the Earth may have been spared.

———

Moonpeople

Essentially nobody on Earth believes today that life can exist on the Moon. However, as I studied the Moon photos by the *Apollo* astronauts, in 2014, I came to the conclusion that there are, in fact, plants and animals, even people, on the Moon. Although the people in most of the *Apollo* images were all quite tiny, some photos of the Moon from NASA gave me the suspicion that there were gigantic people as well. My observations of the Moon with my own camera (Canon SX60), in 2015 and 2016, confirmed my suspicion as I saw that the Moon is now completely covered with people of various sizes, including super giants, on the order of 100 miles tall. Some examples of Moonpeople images follow.

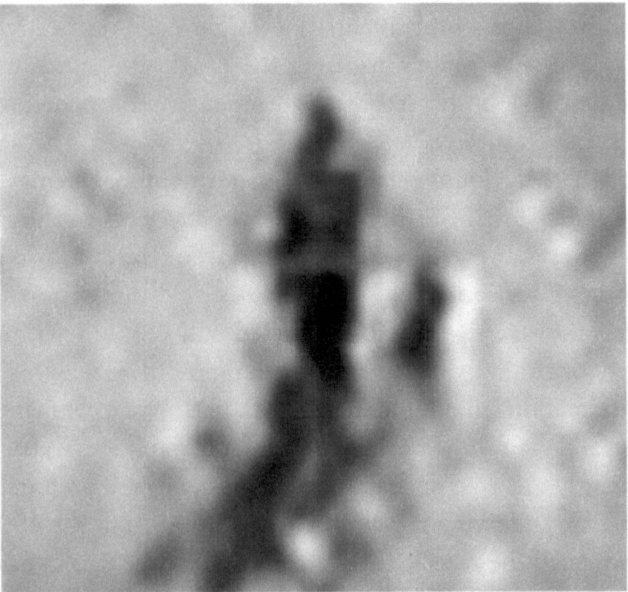

90 MILES TALL MAN WALKING DOG ON MOON SURFACE

This appears to be a man with a red shirt and black pants, walking with what may be a dog, across the surface of the Moon. Scaling the man's height, in proportion to the Moon's diameter, gives his height as 90 miles. I took this picture with my own digital camera.

MINI MOONPEOPLE WATCHING APOLLO ASTRONAUTS

From *Apollo 17*, tiny people were sitting on rocks, watching the astronauts. Apparently, the astronauts were too busy to notice or were somewhat blinded by the bright light.

Hillpeople

The Earth was at one time, perhaps hundreds of millions of years ago and perhaps as recent as 10 million years ago, covered with people as the Moon is today. And because of a passing of the Earth through Jupiter's atmosphere, the Earth people were all instantly frozen and eventually petrified and siliconized. The people that I am seeing in rocks, people of various sizes, were seemingly ever present all over the Earth as they were in Chonosuke Okamura's Japanese mountains, in British rocks, in Hawaii, and throughout the Americas. Within rocks, it seems, with some few exceptions, are the petrified remains of people. But what dawned on me, on April 22, 2016, was that the giants such as appear almost wall-to-wall, covering portions the Moon, at some time in the distant past, covered the Earth. And therefore, by deduction, they must be visible in photos of the Earth, i.e., Google Earth. I first studied more carefully the Indian Head in Canada, which, evidently, is a complete mystery, something that scientists avoid like the plague and, thus, know nothing about. Having seen that there were many cases of faces and whole bodies of various size in that Google photo of the Indian Head, I turned to my own neighborhood near Fremont, California, on Google Earth. My suspicions were met with success, and I consider this a personal discovery.

What I see is the petrified heads of people and also whole bodies of smaller people on the surface of the ground in my vicinity. These, in my opinion, are representations of the people from long ago, perhaps from Silurian age and perhaps more recent. We know they could be about 200 million years old, which is the approximate time that the hills in that area, the East Bay Hills, rose from beneath what we now know as sea level. One "head" is from the area just above the "E" on the "NILES" sign. That sign scales roughly 30 feet in height, and the head scales about one-third of the height of the "E," which makes it approximately 10 feet in height. That would put his overall height at about 60 feet, using an approximation that head height is roughly six times overall height for people in general.

My thinking is that the people were frozen instantly, most likely from a pass through the atmosphere of Jupiter. Then a great flood submerged them, and the process of petrification occurred. During the flood period, which is a brief one-hundred-thousand-year period, that could have occurred sometime following the freeze. I imagine they became flooded, embedded in the sediment, and only their heads protrude above the sediment today. Later, approximately 140–200 million years ago, the layer that they were deposited in was uplifted from seismic activity to become what we now experience as the hills of the East Bay.

Coinpeople

Similar to rockpeople, there are people in coins, "coinpeople." I have no logical explanation of how people's images can be in coins. Are there minimen living in the U.S. mints? Why are they not affected by the high temperatures? Coins are annealed at high near-melt temperatures before stamping them.

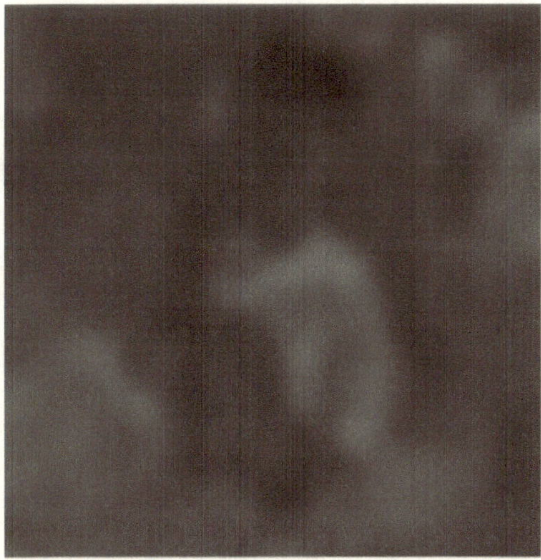

MINIBOY IN OVERALLS IN 1956 D. U.S.CENT

In my search for mint error coins I found one U.S. cent from the Philadelphia mint that had what look like miniman footprints. The size of the footprints is roughly 3 mm, and they appear to be left and right judging the inside arch locations, suggesting a human-like footprint. The stride is consistent with the proportion of human foot size to stride, about four times. The size of the footprints suggests a human roughly 20mm tall with a stride of 13mm, quite within the proportions of human foot/stride ratio while running or jumping.

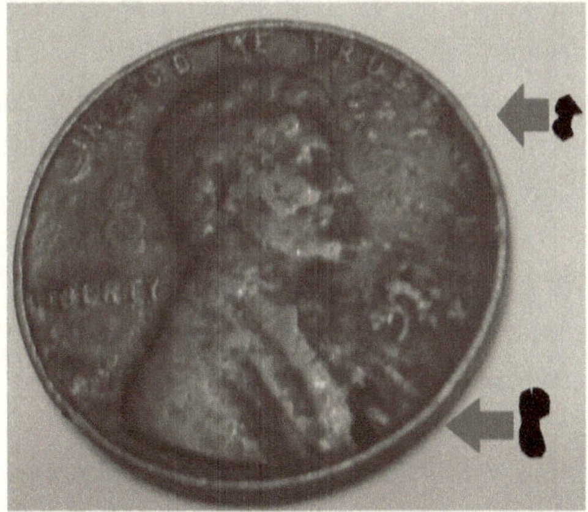

U.S. CENT 1944 WITH
MINIMAN FOOTPRINTS

3

───────

Petrifaction

Most rockpeople images appear to be the product of a process called petrifaction.

Petrifaction is the process in which organic matter becomes saturated and replaced on a molecular level with silica. A common source of silica is volcanic material. In this process, most of the original organic matter is destroyed. Silicification most often occurs in sediments of deltas and flood plains. Water must be present for silicification to occur because it reduces the amount of oxygen present and, therefore, reduces the deterioration of the organism by fungi, maintains organism shape, and allows for the transportation and deposition of silica. The process begins when a specimen is permeated with an aqueous silica solution. The cell walls of the specimen are progressively dissolved and silica is deposited into the empty spaces. In wood samples, as the process proceeds, cellulose and lignin, two components of wood, are degraded and replaced with silica. The specimen is transformed to stone, a process called lithification, as water is lost. For silicification to occur, the geothermic conditions must include a neutral to slightly-acidic pH and a temperature and pressure similar to shallow-depth sedimentary environments; under these conditions, silicification can occur in fifty thousand years or less.

The minipeople we observe in rocks are, therefore, at least fifty thousand years old simply because that much time is needed for the process of petrifaction to occur. This puts them in the approximate time frame of the first *Homo sapiens sapiens*, who came upon the scene sometime around two hundred thousand years ago. Precisely how, when, and where this happened is unknown, although theoretically, as explained in the previous chapter, *Homo sapiens* evolved from *Homo erectus* in Africa and migrated from North Africa through the Middle East, to Europe. There, he came in contact with Neanderthal species, which had earlier, similarly and theoretically, branched from the *Homo erectus* and lived in Europe from roughly two hundred thousand until thirty thousand years ago.

However, the rockpeople found in rocks are older than even the oldest known ancestor of *Homo sapiens*. It would be logical to presume that they are unrelated to *Homo sapiens* because of the obvious conflict in timing. However, because they appear in many ways to be physically so similar to *Homo sapiens*, it is difficult to say with conviction that they are an unrelated species.

Examples of this type of process are rocks in which the images or petrifaction subjects appear to have been embedded into the rock, such as sandstone, quartz, igneous rocks, crystals, and granite.

Silification

There is a secondary process of image creation which is essentially the same thing, except the product is notable for its generally white appearance like quartz. The only difference seems to be the quality of the silica and the presence or absence of other minerals. In this process, it appears that it occurs on top of a previous petrification or lithification material. From the observation of two different processes, the implication is that there were two different events, different but similar nature, that caused each process. The first process caused the rocklike matrix such as serpentine. The second process, at a later time then applied a silified layer on top of the first. The cover photo shows an example of what I call silification.

Rustification

A third process, which causes a slightly-different effect but similar to silification, is the process that results in a rusty appearance. The example below is a dolphin image deposited on the rock surface. The image appears similar to the silification images, in that it is as if a dolphin image is lying on top of a matrix stone, sandstone. It is as if the matrix material occurred during one phase, and the rustlike image was laid upon it in another phase.

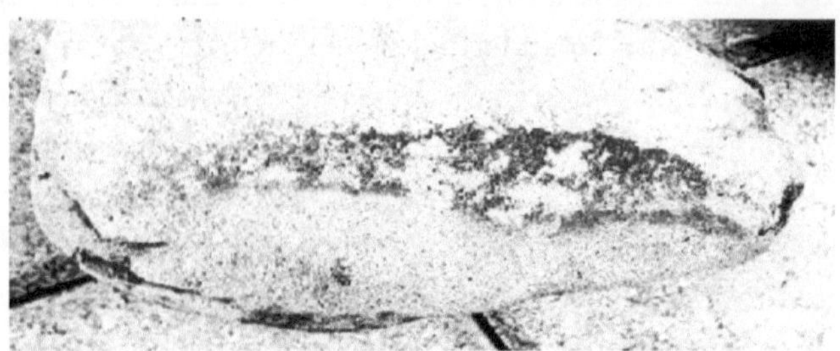

6 INCH MINI-DOLPHIN, NILES, CALIFORNIA

Instant Freezing

Planets' orbits became elliptical because of the passing of a star or sunpartner, a large solar body, near our solar system. The planets with slower orbital velocity travel in more elliptical orbits, thereby overlapping the orbits of other planets and coming close at times. This happens on a periodic basis as our Sun's sunpartners theoretically orbit about our Sun.

From the view of humans on Earth, the approach of the sunpartner may be visible, similar to a comet. For most people, it would be unnoticeable for years, and only upon getting close to our Sun would it become noticeable. It would be as if we had two suns, but one would be dim. An adept astronomer might begin to understand what was happening. Other planets' orbits would change, and at times the "wanderers" would get bigger and brighter and closer to Earth than normal. Mars and Jupiter would be most notable. And finally, out of mathematical inevitability, there would be near collisions with catastrophic happenstance.

And so the tiny blue planet Earth, a fraction of the size of Jupiter, less than 1 percent the size of the immense largest planet of our solar system, could pass through the Jovian atmosphere, at minus 300 degrees Fahrenheit, for over an hour in duration. And all living matter on Earth would have been instantly frozen.

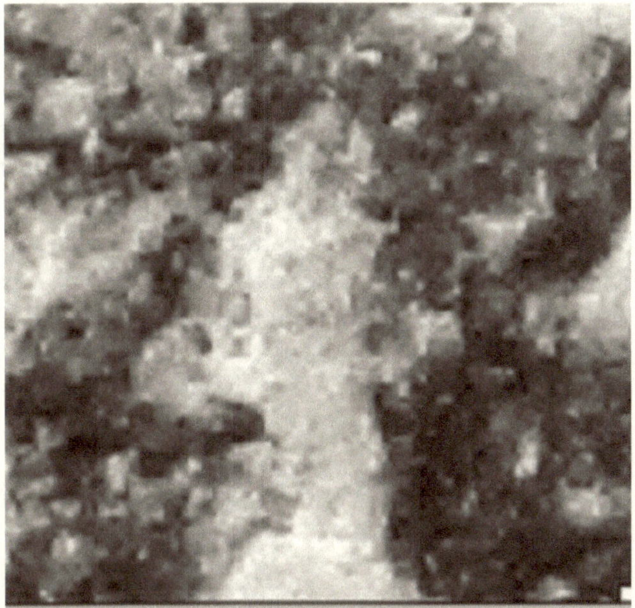

MINIWOMAN SCREAMING, FREMONT, CALIFORNIA

Flooding

Earth's great blue cover, water, before and after freezing, would redistribute by the laws of gravity toward the gigantic planet Jupiter, causing an oblong shape to the normally-spherical body. Floods of immense proportion would be not only attracted to the greater gravity but then frozen on the side closest to Jupiter. Slowly, over hundreds or thousands of years, the water would melt and go back to its oceans, lakes, and rivers, where it belongs.

Lithification

The process of lithification occurs as silica, the most abundant element on Earth, dissolves in water and gradually deposits in layers upon layers as the water evaporates.

Petrification

As the silica deposits and the water evaporated over millennia and uncountable cycles, petrification occurs. Molecule by molecule of organic matter becomes replaced by silica, the transparent crystalline material that preserves the ancient forms that were once frozen, flooded, and lithified. And the bodies of what were living creatures became solidified in stone, not only in form but also in color. And so not only were they petrified, but also their last seconds of motion and emotion were recorded for all time.

4

Rock Animals

My findings include animals as well, not just extinct dinosaur creatures, but also miniature versions of animals from the African continent, in rocks from the North American continent, such as rhinoceros, somewhat miniature in size, less than a foot in overall length. In fact, fossils of extinct rhinoceros species, *Teleoceras*, have been found in North America from the Miocene epoch, roughly five thousand to fifteen thousand years ago. The *Teleoceras* were large, similar to modern rhinos, but with shorter legs, one horn, and semi-aquatic, similar to hippopotamus. These rock rhinos from Alameda Creek in Fremont appear to be two-horned, similar to African rhinos today, although much smaller. The photo below shows the head of a rhino about two inches from nose to neck, a rustification on sandstone, probably 100 million years old or more.

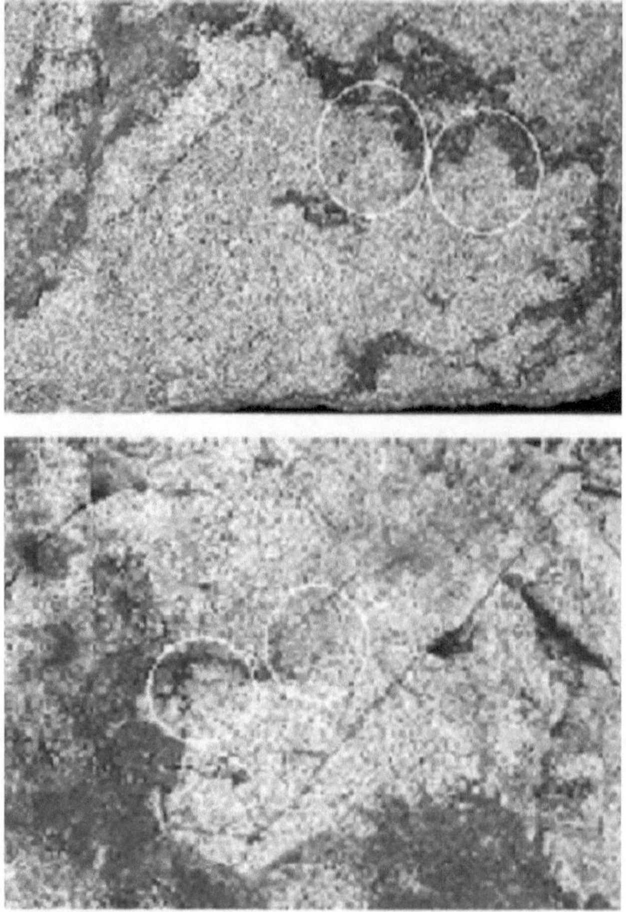

TWO HORNED RHINOS, FREMONT, CALIFORNIA

Undoubtedly, these animals dated from the times of the supercontinent of Pangea, which existed hundreds of millions of years ago, when the North American continent was connected to the continent of Africa. However, the rhinoceros species we know today is known to have originated only about 50 million years ago.

The supercontinent of Pangea begun to break up 300 million years ago. North and South America subsequently and gradually drifted westward.

MOOSE ON GRANITE, FREMONT, CALIFORNIA

Enlargement shows a hippopotamus with a woman's face. The hippopotamus evolved around 60 million years ago. The process seems to be a combination of silification and rustification and is similar to the rhino images, above, and the seagull, below.

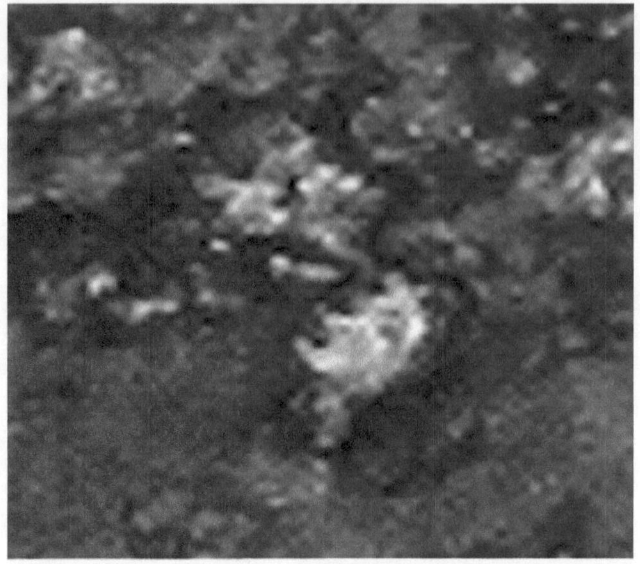

HIPPO ALONGSIDE A MINIWOMAN'S HEAD

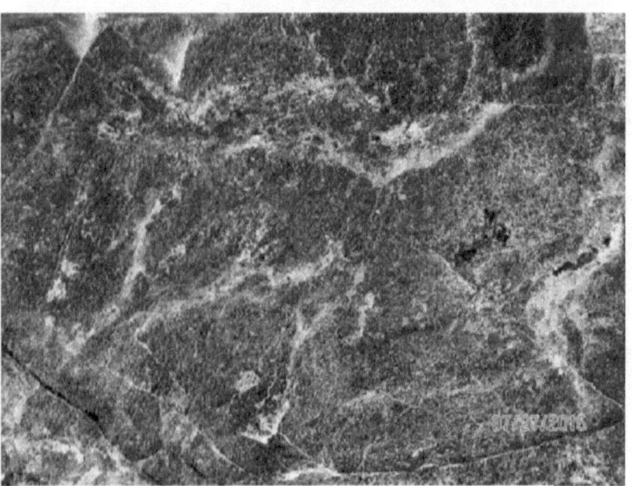

SEAGULL, BERKELEY, CALIFORNIA

Seagull image from rock at entrance to Berkeley Pier, Berkeley, California. Seagulls originated around 30–33 million years ago.

Dolphins are mammals that originated around 48 million years ago, from an animal with legs, called *Archaeoceti*. The mini-dolphin, shown as a rustification, would seem to have been older based on dating estimates.

MINI-DINOSAUR, JAWS AROUND HUMAN, IN A PEBBLE

ELEPHANT, NILES CANYON, FREMONT, CALIFORNIA

Silification of elephant and man, above. The elephant head is about three inches across. The man's head is about one. Elephants originated around 66 million years ago.

5

Dating

I have little confidence regarding the dating of the rock images I have examined. They do, however, seem to be from various processes and ages. Okamura speculated that rockpeople were frozen and petrified at one great event in the Silurian age, 400 million years ago, with a single process, but my findings are that there have been many instances or events occurring at irregular intervals and under different processes and circumstances. Using radioactive decay methods of dating would be probably helpful, although I am unable to obtain assistance in any way from anyone in that area. I would date-test the rocks if I could. Even that would be questionable, however, because the rock might have been formed millions of years prior to the deposit of an image upon it, in cases of silifications or rustifications. Even rocks with embedded silified images of people, such as granite, contain a matrix and the objects embedded in the matrix. So age-dating might be giving age of matrix rather than the people in the matrix, thus not accurately revealing what the true age of the people is.

Because my attempts to date the rocks by associating with early species of man, as I review in Chapter 7, "Evolution of Mankind," proved completely futile, and the use of evolution of various animals as a method of dating is equally futile, and since the evidence shows mankind existed long prior to Earth's evolutionary life cycle, which lasted during the past 600 million years or so, I can only make a loose estimate of the ages of the various rocks I have examined. I can say, with some confidence, that people and animals in rock images seem to predate modern evolution as seen in Chonosuke Okamura's findings, as well as my own examination of meteorites, Earth's oldest rocks, and Moon rocks.

As I described in the previous, Chapter 3, "Petrifaction," there are many different processes that occurred. There are embedment of seemingly-petrified people such as in granite and limestone, and there are surface deposits such as silifications and rustifications on sandstone and serpentine and lava or magma. The embedded petrification, in which images appear almost like photographs, seem to be much more highly detailed than the silifications, which are more like roadkill that has been deformed, compressed, and dehydrated. Are they from different events? Or were they simply different because they underwent different environmental changes? My guess is that they were from different times and events.

The humanlike images, generally, allowing for distortion brought about by processes, look clearly the same as ourselves, *Homo sapiens*. There is no sign of prehuman form, such as *Australopithecus afarensis* or *Homo erectus*, with brow ridges or hairy bodies or concave noses. All are wearing clothes as we make from fabrics. There are a variety of sizes and shapes, although they appear to be consistent with our own body and facial shapes, which vary similarly. Facial hair is like our own, with beards and mustaches, sometimes mustaches without beards, implying shaving. Wearable styles and similar items, like clothing, hats, or sunglasses, seem to vary widely, from ancient to modern and even ethnically, from East to West, and thus cannot be used as a basis for dating. If the time span of our "behaviorally modern" *Homo sapiens* is considered to be only in the approximate time of one hundred thousand years (the oldest fossils of "anatomically modern" humans may go back four hundred thousand years), then the ages of people in rocks obviously go back much, much farther in time. In fact, one needs to question whether the scientific findings are perhaps erroneous; after all, they are based only upon the limited quantity of available fossils, while the amount of rock specimens available for images is essentially infinite.

Meteorites with images of people, microscopic in size, date from millions, even billions, of years ago, during the solar system formation.

Pangea Supercontinent

As we now understand, the Pangea breakup, a very slow and gradual movement of geologic plates separation, occurred about 300 million years ago. The Americas were contiguous with Africa until then. Thus, the presence of images of African-continent animals (rhinos, elephants, hippopotami) in stones in Western North America indicate that the stone images of those animals could be at least that old or even older. Okamura believed the minipeople in Japanese granite were formed in the Silurian period, over 400 million years ago, which seems to support that the rockpeople in the Americas experienced an event at that time as well. However, it has to be reckoned that the events and/or processes that turned the people to stone could have occurred after the Pangea breakup as well as before it as the continents drifted apart. The animals could have existed for long periods before and/or after the breakup as the breakup might have been a very gradual process, not catastrophic, and not related to the freeze event.

RHINO, FOOTBALL SIZE, ALAMEDA CREEK, CALIFORNIA

Rhino, overall length about a foot, rustification on serpentine, Alameda Creek, Fremont, California. Current evolution of the rhino is estimated at 30–40 million years ago (early Eocene). Also, there are fossils showing that rhinos existed in North America at that time. However, such fossils were much larger than these, although smaller than existing species, and therefore, the time of existence of those fossils cannot be considered the same as the rhino's in these silifications. My guess is that the rhinos in my studies are younger than Pangea and older than the Eocene fossils, therefore in the 30–300, and possibly more precisely 100–200, million years range in age.

East Bay

Berkeley Hills and San Francisco Bay Area rocks, according to geological reports, date to less than 200 million years ago, having lifted through seismic activity. Although that is possibly consistent with Okamura's Silurian period as the time of the event freezing minimen, it suggests that there might have been more than one period of instant global freezing. One possibility is that we are looking at 400 million-year-old rocks that were buried then uplifted to the surface 200 million years ago. Even in the San Francisco East Bay rocks, however, there was a volcanic event at Sibley, which spewed lava only 10 million years ago, and rocks from those areas, containing people images, suggest that there was a freezing event at or sometime after that period.

Sandstone from Albany Hill in the East San Francisco Bay Area, which geologists explain as part of the Franciscan Assembly, likewise date from as recent as the Jurassic period, 200 million years ago. They do reveal human forms in microscopic size, although various, similar to what Chonosuke Okamura discovered in Japan. The photo of two pebbles from Albany Hill, below, demonstrates some of the faces of various-sized people with hats, clothing, sunglasses, and dogs:

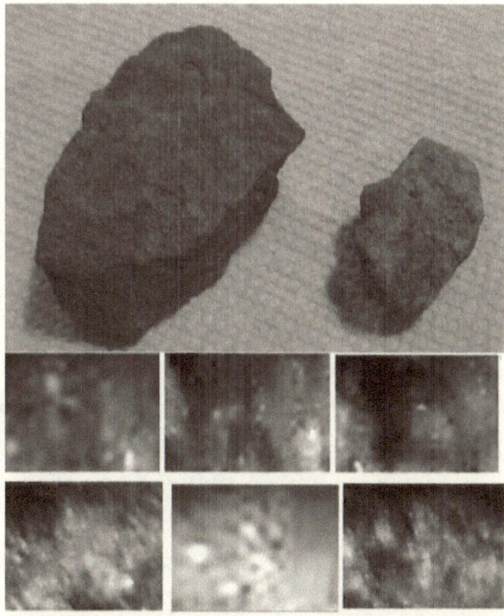

ALBANY HILL, CALIFORNIA. ROCKS ARE FROM FRANCISCAN
ASSEMBLAGE. 200 MYA, HATS, SUNGLASSES, DOGS

In the Niles Canyon area of East Bay hills, there is the local sandstone that seems similar to granite, just smaller grain size. The sandstone contains people that vary in size, from microscopic to finger size and even larger, similar to river rock granite. There are larger formations within granite boulders that show people in the range of six inches to a foot high. Other local rocks, such as the serpentine rocks, which were used to line the banks of the Alameda Creek flood channel, seem to have a combination of microscopic people embedded in the serpentine with what looks like squashed layers of white silification people on the surface. Are the negative images of the same age as the positive, and are the siliconized people the same age as the embedded? Then there are rustifications, such as the rhino and dolphin examples (see chapter on "Rock Animals"), which is an entirely different process. Are the different processes from different events? There is generally an understanding that the rocks from the Niles Canyon area formed during the Knoxville Formation, which dates to roughly 150 million years ago (late Jurassic period). The Niles Canyon rocks, sandstone and granite, seem to be from a period 50 million years after the Franciscan Assembly, Albany Hills, of 200 million years age. So the rustifications and silifications of the Fremont area appear to be from a period earlier than the Albany Hill sandstones, possibly 150 million years old.

Mount Lassen

There were many eruptions at Mount Lassen over the past 30 million years. Although I did detect rockpeople in the rocks from the area, I do not know exactly what period the rocks came from. The horses, silifications on the surface of a lava boulder, alongside the road, in a field strewn by similar boulders, suggest that they were possibly distributed by glaciers after their formation. I would estimate the age of formation of these images is, therefore, around 30 million years ago soon after the volcanic eruption period. Horses evolved, by comparison, approximately 45–55 million years ago from an animal called Eohippus. Modern horses were believed to have originated in North America within the past 5 million years, and they migrated. However, these images appear more like small modern-day horses, rather than the extinct midsize North American species. And of course, they were much smaller, like a foot-tall Arabian.

MINI-HORSES, MOUNT LASSEN, CALIFORNIA

Sibley Regional Volcanic Preserve

Sibley Volcanic Preserve is a site in the hills above Berkeley, California. The volcano was active about 10 million years ago and is one of the few areas where the age of the rocks is tested and known from Argon-Potassium radioactive decay tests. Images of rockpeople from rocks within the Sibley caldera indicate that there must have been a freeze event within the past 10 million years, most likely soon before the time of eruption. The rock is a red lava-type stone with the people seemingly integral to the rock, that is not "on" it but "in" it. The people form the rock. It is as if the people are "frozen" in their positions, not affected by the volcanic heat or flow, and thus, they must have been frozen prior to the eruption, not during or after. This seems to be a process entirely different from all previous examples I have observed. How could the people freeze and yet be within a lava flow without being incinerated? It seems possible only if they were petrified as well before the eruption.

I examined different types of rock in the area, including a red lava type, a red lava with a rustification layer, and what seems like more ancient rocks of basalt. They all contain rockpeople images.

One red lava rock from the Sibley caldera shows clearly a woman in a red dress, dark hair, beside a horse-like animal. She measures about one-sixteenth inch in height, with even smaller people near her.

Another rock from the same caldera area has a reddish-colored rustification/silification layer on the surface of red and sometimes gray base. Brochures at the reserve explain that the reddish-colored features on the surface of the rock are caused by steam acting on the rock. The rocks exhibit images of rockpeople throughout the rustifications as well as throughout the matrix. One example shows a man's face, with dark brown hair, mustache, and Caucasian features. Only his head is visible, as if the body is submerged in the rock. Other faces and smaller bodies and animals can be seen around his, which stands out for some unknown reason.

An enlargement from the same rock shows a couple sitting on a rock, with a man in black coat and hat passing by in the foreground on the right, looking at them. The man seems to have a hat like a leprechaun, while the woman has a green dress and is sitting with her legs across his.

Another example from Sibley is probably an ancient rock found outside the caldera, a small piece that fractured from the top of a huge boulder. This was probably an "ancient" rock because of its gray color, unlike the red lava rocks, as well as the size of the boulder it came from, which was roughly a three-foot cube in size. The rockpeople in that case were wearing sunglasses. Two same-size men's faces were next to each other. Bodies were embedded in the stone.

Hawaiian Island of Oahu

The photo below is from a rock in Hawaii, from the rock wall of the Waikiki Post Office. The rocks are presumed to be local, from the island, as they appear volcanic, like pumice. Of course, they could be imported, but then it does not seem practical for anyone to import rocks to an island full of rocks. The photo shows a man with a brimmed hat, boots, and a sort of Scottish kilt. He seems to also have a breastplate and possibly a device on his back, quite possibly bagpipes. They seem to be talking to a man inside a hole in the rock. Since the island of Oahu was formed by volcanic eruptions about 3 million years ago (2.6 Mount Koolau to 3.6 Mount Waianae), it suggests that the petrification process occurred at some time after that time. Looking at a geomagnetic reversal chart, there were several reversals that occurred during that period, and so the exact time of the freeze cannot be determined, except that it can be estimated that a freeze had to have occurred sometime during the past 3 million years, obviously much more recent than Okamura's 400-million-year-old Japanese limestone minimen. This conclusion suggests that such freeze events are much more frequent, occurring within millions of years, not hundreds of millions of years, apart. And of course, modern history, being less than ten thousand years of age, has no record of them.

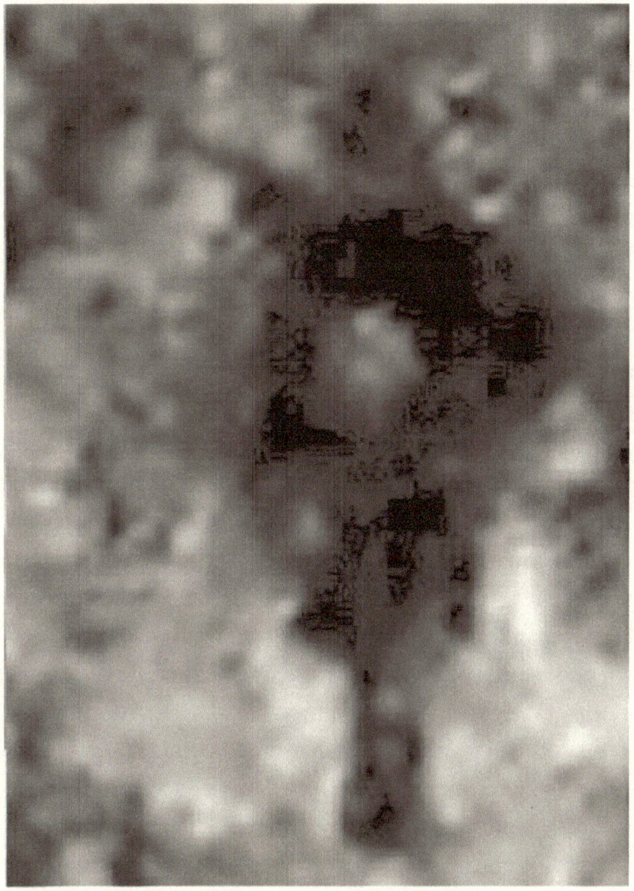

MINI-SCOTTSMAN WITH KILT, BAGPIPES, OAHU, HAWAII

Geomagnetic Reversals

Another perspective on dating might be gleaned from geomagnetic reversals. The cause of reversals is unknown and debated, with many explanations. One possible explanation is that an interplanetary approach without actually colliding with Earth, by a planet or other large solar system body with a strong geomagnetic field, could cause reversal or movement of Earth's poles, just as two magnets held together tend to attract opposite poles. Although Mars has a very weak and relatively-insignificant magnetic system, Jupiter has a very strong magnetic pole system, and therefore, it is a likelier cause of reversals. The reversals of Earth's poles during the past 5 million years are known to have occurred from geomagnetic studies.

The current period in which the poles are as they are now is called the Brunhes Chron, which began 780,000 years ago. There was a brief reversal 41,000 years ago, called the Laschamp Event, which lasted only 440 years. A recent reversal chart only goes back 5 million years, but the pole reversals of Earth have been thoroughly studied for hundreds of millions of years by examining ice at Earth's poles. The Sibley volcanic activity, for example, 10 million years ago, cannot be placed on a recent chart as it exceeds the 5-million-year period. The only example that I have seen that falls within this chart is the hypothetical Hawaiian island freeze event, which occurred around 3 million years ago, when the Hawaiian island of Oahu formed. The reversal chart does support that hypothesis as it shows a reversal during that period from roughly 2.6–3.1 million years ago. In other words, the Hawaiian islands might have been formed at the same time and possibly as a consequence of a large mass approaching Earth around 3 million years ago. The population of rockpeople then accumulated on Oahu over a period of hundreds of thousands of years, and then those people experienced a great freeze event, perhaps at the end of the reversal, 2.6 million years ago.

The reversal chart indicates that geomagnetic reversals are fairly common and occur frequently, lasting less than a million years, generally, and sometimes include several brief reversals within longer periods. Since written historical records, such as clay tablets, cover less than ten thousand years at best, and because of the short period of the chart, 5 million years, it does not help much in dating rocks in which human images are found by this author, except for those from Oahu. The formation of the island apparently occurred during the Gauss Chron and, to be more specific, during the three brief periods within the Gauss Chron, around 2.6–3.6 million years ago.

The Laschamp Event, forty-one thousand years ago, was brief in nature. Cause is unknown. Its relevance is that it occurred at about the time that mankind was evolving in terms of language and social activity.

Clothing, which is believed to have been the cause of loss of body hair, is believed to have come into use around seventy thousand years ago. Language, developed along with social structure, such as communities or towns and cities, is believed to have developed after that or around the same time. The "archaic humans" of one hundred thousand to two hundred thousand years ago may not have language or speaking as we know it. They may have had small vocabularies and gestures like apes, which today seem capable of learning dozens of "words" or "verbalized expressions," which they communicate with sign language, sounds, and facial expressions. The oldest known anatomically-modern "archaic" human fossils have been found in the Eastern and Southern Mediterranean/North African areas, approximately one hundred thousand years old. Some dating suggests they may be from four hundred thousand years ago, even before Neanderthals. Oldest known Caucasian fossils were found in North Africa and dated to forty-five thousand years old, having Neanderthal DNA of higher proportion than today's Europeans. The first "white-skinned" Caucasian fossils date to forty thousand years old in Southern Russia. Hence, the sketchy evidence seems to suggest that the white Caucasian race evolved almost precisely at or near the time of the Laschamp Event. Pole reversals are associated with reduction in magnetic pole protection from solar radiation, and hence, it is believed that during the short time of the Laschamp Event, which lasted about 440 years, about twenty human generations, there was more-than-usual cosmic radiation on Earth, resulting in more-than-normal genetic variation. But in another explanation, if pole reversals occur because of interplanetary approaches, the transfer of humans from another solar system body, such as Mars, the Moon, or something else, at that time, is a possibility. The Laschamp Event seems to have occurred simultaneously with the early beginnings of modern civilization.

Clothing, Sunglasses, and Hat Styles

Some of the rockpeople seem to wear sunglasses and other types of clothing. The idea occurred to me that the clothing might be used to help date them. Clothing styles appear modern. Some are nineteenth century, but most appear late twentieth century in style.

The images show that some people in rocks wore sunglasses as far back as 400 million years ago. Even the image of a man on a Moon rock, possibly over 4 billion years old, appears to wear sunglasses. Historically, however, they were invented after the development of glass production, in 15th century AD, and became used in the mid-1700s, although for medical purposes. They didn't become popular until the early 1900s (by Earthlings). It implies that the star from which humans originated was dimmer than our Sun, which, therefore, causes us even today to have difficulty with the Sun's brightness.

6

Rockpeople

Behavior

Rockpeople appear to be not only anatomically identical to ourselves, except size, but also exhibiting behavioral similarity. They might be considered a type of *Homo sapiens* species, as Chonosuke Okamura assigned, except for the fact that they are clearly of significantly various sizes, tiny and gigantic, as well as our size. That fact makes me believe that we are simply a specific size of the multisized species. It would not make sense to me to call every size a different species.

Behaviorally, what is observable in the images within rocks is their clothing, their houses, their cars, and other miscellaneous objects that demonstrate a high degree of variation in style, ethnicity, and also industrial and technological ability, just as what exists today. An image of their houses show them to be uncannily like our own. Of course, the houses are tiny little things, a fraction of an inch in height. They had ethnic and racial differences similar to *Homo sapiens* Earthlings today. This particular rock is granite from Niles Canyon in Fremont, California, and is, by my dating estimate, 140 million years old. Even today scientists do not use different species names for different sized people such as pigmies or giants.

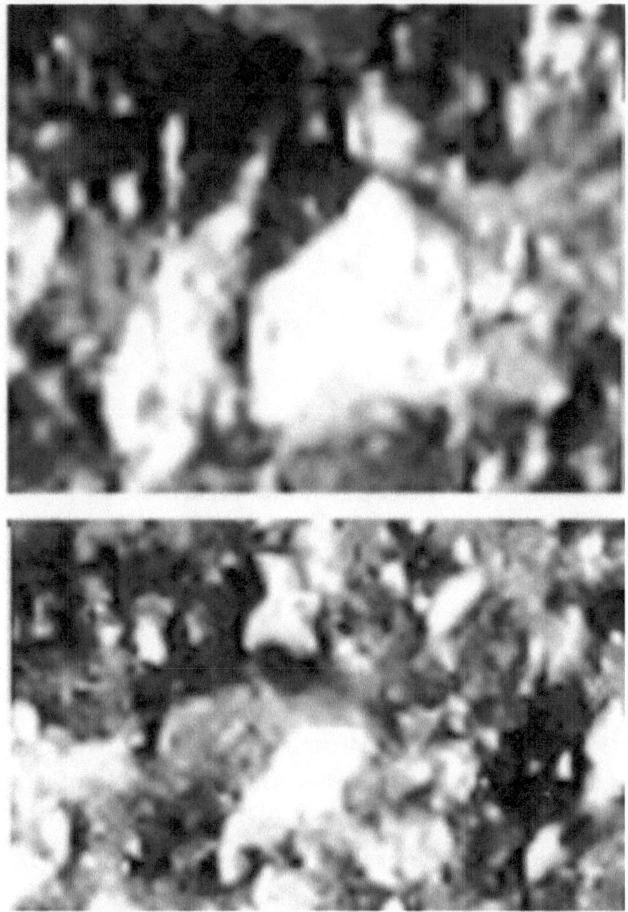

MINI-HOUSES, NILES CANYON, CALIFORNIA

In fact, they are so much like us that one has to wonder, how could it be that we are *not* their descendants or related to them in some way? The image below gives an idea of the various sizes or rockpeople. Often several sizes of people can be seen in the same image. Tiny people are accompanied by yet tinier people, and bigger people frequently can be seen with tiny people on their shoulders or in their hats. In the following example, as the "bigger" man's face on the left is about one inch across, the tiny people on his hat are just a fraction of that size. The tiny man with a cap seems to hold another person's head in his lap, a woman whose head is several times larger than the little man's, and even smaller people yet seem to be in the image.

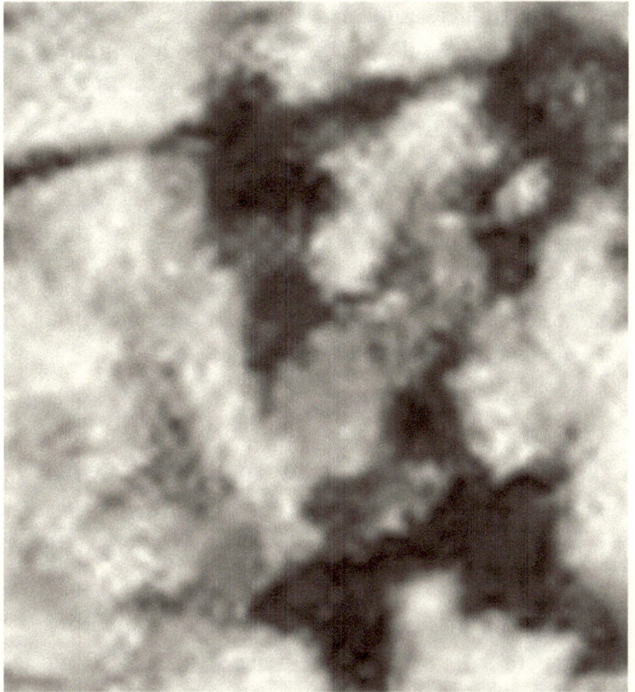

MINIMAN IN GRANITE, NILES CANYON, CALIFORNIA

The size variability of the rockpeople is consistent with that which I have observed on Mars and the Moon. And it seems a part of their behavior that people of all sizes seem to live among one another. Larger people seem to "carry" tiny people on their shoulders. They may even consider them as a sort of ornament like the way we think of jewelry. Of course, on Earth, we have no such culture. The uniformity of size of Earthlings today gives us great simplification in our social interactions or at least so it seems.

Continuity with Modern Humans

Evolutionary theory of all living things, not only evolution of mankind, is, upon deep examination, indisputable and, therefore, cannot be contradicted by the evidence of rockpeople as observed and presented herein. Yet the rockpeople appear, in many ways, other than size, to be identical to ourselves. How could that be possible? Two possibilities come to mind, "continuity" and "re-evolution," which, by nature, are contradictory at first glimpse but, in fact, not necessarily so. They could both be valid. If there was a continuity of mankind's existence through hundreds of millions of years, then his re-evolution becomes questionable. On the other hand, if evolution did occur as in current theory, then examples of continuity should not occur in rockpeople images or would be seen very rarely. A break in the continuity of man would imply that all features of man's existence today would be unidentical, different from, those of the rockpeople. And contrarily, if the rockpeople were, indeed, our direct predecessors, our actual ancestors, then there would be indications of that in the images. Therefore, a review of the extent of similarity is useful to ascertain whether we are re-evolved or a continuation.

Several observed examples of continuity suggest that the current human species, *Homo sapiens*, is the same species as those in rocks. Several observed examples of continuity include clothing styles, sunglasses, telescopes, houses, cars, Santa Claus, witch's hat, races white, black, and Asian.

Looking at the photo above of the tiny rockpeople houses, it appears that they constructed them in nearly-identical design to modern houses. They appear to be with red tile roofs and stucco, with rectangular windows, with gable roofs, rectangular in shape. For that to be the case, they needed to have been developed technologically in a manner similar to ourselves, with roofing-tile-manufacturing methods, cement-processing methods, glass, metal fasteners, and so on. It seems unlikely, considering the vast range of housing styles that have occurred with modern man, that people millions of years ago would use such similar construction methods and shapes.

Looking at a photo of man from Chonosuke Okamura's studies, "Related Studies," there is a man with a fur cap and a telescope on his right shoulder. The man's cap is similar to Russian fur caps worn today, and the telescope is similar to telescopes from the 1600s. This sort of evidence of continuity is evident throughout rockpeople images, suggesting that "we" are actually "them" and "they" did not go extinct but somehow transferred or passed down their lifestyles to us.

A 1929 Duesenberg-style vehicle was found on the surface of a granite river boulder in Niles Canyon. The development of automobiles indicates that they had achieved considerable knowledge and technical ability, similar to ours, although on a different scale or size and much prior.

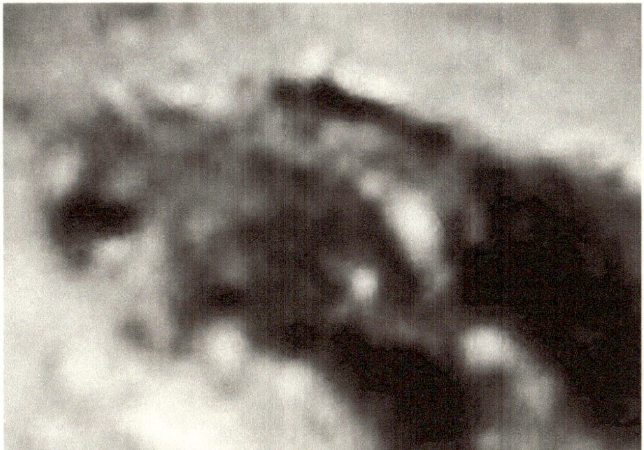

MINI-VEHICLE SIMILAR TO 1929 DEUSENBERG

Other such examples of continuity are a Santa Claus image from a granite river rock and a woman with a witch's hat in a rock with iron pyrite. In fact, most of the hats are extremely similar to modern hats. Furthermore, there is clear evidence in the rockpeople of races as rockpeople appear generally to be Caucasian, with some minority Asians and Blacks. Clothing styles among rockpeople seem a mixture of various ethnicities, styles, and periods, although they seem mostly to be modern as we wear today. There are no people in the rock images that appear like cave men wearing furs, such as those depicted by artists in rendering cave-dweller early men. There is at least one example of an American Indian head dress in the Canadian Indian Head Monument. "Related Studies." So American Indians existed in the distant past, even before evolution of modern man?

The multitude of examples of evidence support the concept of continuity. As for the concept of re-evolution, there is some evidence that supports that as well, the strongest of which is evolutionary theory itself. Looking carefully at the evolution of mankind as he apparently evolved, as evidenced by fossils and recent scientific discoveries, show a steady, continual progress from ape to man, in growth of cranium size, development of behavioral patterns, such as language, writing, music, apparel manufacture and design, technological developments, such as the wheel, and ultimately, the entire known archeological and artistic record. So both theories, continuity and re-evolution, are supported by substantial evidence. The two concepts seem to represent a dichotomy, two things opposed or entirely different. Yet both appear possible.

There is one other third concept that might explain what truly happened: interplanetary exchange. An interplanetary exchange event may have occurred that led to Earthlings' final development, behavior, i.e., language, writing, music, and social development. So we have not a dichotomy but a trichotomy, and each of the three concepts, evolution, re-evolution, and interplanetary exchange, can be true or untrue. The biblical stories of the Nephilim, the giants who fell from the sky at the time of Noah, lend credence to the concept of interplanetary exchange.

Origin

The evidence seen in rockpeople images conflicts with the modern theory of evolution. It demonstrates that humankind existed long before the theoretical evolutionary origins of modern human beings, within the past two hundred thousand years, for anatomically-similar modern humans, and fifty thousand years for known socially-, intellectually-developed, behaviorally-similar, humans. The appearance of images of human-like figures wearing clothing, sunglasses, and hats like our own on ancient rocks hundreds of millions and even billions or more years old suggests that the origin of humanity was before the formation of the Earth and the Moon and, thus, before the beginning of our solar system.

The Sun's solar system formation is quite precisely estimated to have begun 4.568 billion years ago. The Moon has been similarly estimated as having formed 4.527 billion years ago, 30–50 million years after the formation of the solar system. Earth's formation is estimated as having occurred 4.54 billion years ago, plus or minus 50 million years, which puts it around the same time as the Moon's formation. And thus, by these estimates, the solar system formed first, followed by the formation of Earth and Moon, probably in that sequence. A rock from the Moon's surface, brought back by *Apollo 15* astronauts, named the Genesis rock, shows a tiny petrified humanoid form sitting on the rock and is dated at 4.46 billion years old. So apparently, this is a rock that formed 100 million years after the Moon and Earth joined or collided, and it has tiny people on it that have been through a "freeze" event and petrification process, which could have occurred anytime afterward.

It is difficult to imagine the origin of humankind at or during the formation of the solar system as the environment must have been quite unlivable. Without a star or Sun, deep space is vacuum and without heat, oxygen, water, or anything that would be necessary for survival. Even the modern evolutionary theory would have difficulty in explaining that humans evolved in the time between formation of the Sun and formation of Earth, approximately 200 million years. Even the oldest known living organisms, such as algae, jellyfish, and worms, are estimated to have formed on Earth as recently as 600 million years ago. The suggestion is that evolution takes many hundreds of millions of years, from origin of simple species to human-like creatures. On Earth, the fossil record shows that it took over half a billion years from first life to human. Therefore, it becomes evident, in fact obvious, through the time estimates of the solar system and evolutionary studies, that the origins of humankind preceded that of the solar system and, therefore, came about long before it, perhaps hundreds of millions or billions of years before, from somewhere outside our solar system. Therefore, humankind is not only "extraterrestrial," but also "extra-stellar," and apparently came from a star system somewhere outside our solar system. This conflicts harshly with modern evolutionary theory and even brings it deeply into question. If evolutionary theory is flawed, then something apparently happened one hundred thousand to two hundred thousand years ago to bring about modern humans on Earth. Unfortunately, the fossil record does not show precisely what happened in that period. Nevertheless, considering the rock images, the modern human species, *Homo sapiens sapiens*, seems to have "appeared" rather than "evolved" at the moment.

Earthlings, by the above reasoning, are one of the following: (1) a re-evolved species, (2) an alien species, or (3) a combination or mixture of a preman species, such as anatomically-similar humans interbred or possibly educated by an alien species. The truth about this subject will only become known if we are ultimately able to analyze carefully the forms of humankind from places other than Earth, such as those that appear on Mars and the Moon and other solar system bodies. If we could extract the DNA from a Moonperson or Martian, for example, we could determine their relationship with Earthlings. The evidence presented herein is admittedly meager, limited to fuzzy enlargements and distorted image-capturing processes. The beings I observe on the Moon and Mars and other solar system bodies appear to be very similar to Earthlings in both form and behavior, discounting, of course, the size differences. However, they are living in outer space or in environments that Earthlings could not withstand or so it seems. Yet it seems too coincidental or, in other words, unlikely, near impossible, that the same human form would evolve in various environments under different gravity, different atmosphere, different diet, different radiological conditions, different degrees of exposure to sunlight, different natural catastrophes, etc. Therefore, it is important at this juncture, with Earthlings stretching out their reach to other worlds, to study carefully the differences among beings from various places other than Earth. And the first step, unfortunately, which has yet to be taken, is to simply accept that life exists elsewhere outside of Earth. It does seem that we are on the verge, however, of that determination, considering recent exploration.

7

Human Evolution

According to current theory, when did the human species begin, and where did the first modern human being, *Homo sapiens sapiens*, come from? Nobody knows for sure, and of course, there is controversy about those questions. Actually, our written historical record goes back only around five thousand years, and not much is known before that. Even archaeological records, such as cave paintings, go back only about twenty thousand years to the earliest records of human society. And anthropological records show that humans evolved over the past 5 million years, from primates, likely chimpanzees. Zoologists and paleoanthropologists are quite ingrained with Darwin's theory of evolution and have unearthed fossils that support the theory solidly and in detail. The slow but steady evolution from chimp to human seems to have passed through stages, from apelike chimp predecessor (Ida) to *Australopithecus africanus*, (Lucy), to Australopithecus Erectus, to archaic humans, such as Homo sapiens neanderthal, to anatomically modern humans, such as Denisovans, and then finally, to us, *Homo sapiens sapiens*. Although there are disagreements among scientists about details and specifics, the general theory of evolution is the basis of their beliefs.

However, in spite of the fact that human species have been found and dated, and a logical progression appears to have occurred, there are gaps in the picture of human evolution, and in fact, new species have never been observed to have evolved in modern records. According to the fossil record, the "moment" of change, the "origin" of *Homo sapiens*, occurred around two hundred thousand to three hundred thousand years ago, when something like a *Homo erectus*, having a larger brain, evolved to *Homo heidelbergensis*, moved out of Africa to Europe and Asia and then evolved to *Homo sapiens*. There is no scientific record or fossil of any *Homo sapiens* before that period other than rockpeople as observed by Okamura. Exactly how and when and where behaviorally-modern humans began is unknown, although theoretical estimates, based on DNA, might put it at the area of North India, around fifty thousand to one hundred thousand years ago. Racial differences are, in theory, the latest evolutionary "change" in mankind, having occurred, supposedly, after migrations to different climactic environments, with different Sun exposures, temperature ranges, topography, wildlife surrounds, water and food availability, etc.

Homo erectus, with earliest fossils dating to 2 million years ago, lived until roughly seventy thousand years ago, existing alongside some early *Homo sapiens*. Use of fire for cooking was first developed by this human ancestor, which is also known as a hunter-gatherer, who traveled in groups, hunted large animals, used primitive tools, and communicated something more sophisticated than the sounds of chimpanzees but much less than language of humans.

There were differences between Homo sapiens neanderthal and *Homo sapiens sapiens*. Neanderthal had an equal and possibly bigger brain and bigger bones. He was shorter and stronger. He seems to have died out, gone extinct, at about the same time as the coming on the scenes of modern mankind, with some overlap, estimated to be from thirty thousand to fifty thousand years ago. Another three prehuman species, the *Homo erectus*, more specifically, Homo floresiencus, on the island of Flores in Indonesia, and Homo sapiens neanderthal, both apparently went extinct at about that time, leaving only modern man. DNA studies show that the modern man interbred with Neanderthal as modern European DNA demonstrates. *Homo erectus*, by projection, might have interbred with anatomically-modern humans as they lived side-by-side in North Africa for a brief period before Erectus became extinct. There is DNA evidence indicating interbreeding between Denisovans and modern humans in Melanesia. Denisovans were discovered in 2010 and are believed to have gone extinct 14,500 years ago. These things are developing today.

The extinction of Neanderthal may have exceptions. There was a case of a possible Neanderthal woman in the 1800s in Russia, who was captured, used as a sex slave, and had offspring, which were, in essence,

Homo sapiens by DNA. So in other words, if there is offspring from Neanderthal woman/sapiens man, the offspring are *Homo sapiens* in DNA. There is no evidence that Neanderthal exists today anywhere on Earth. One wild man in a cave might have been killed in a cave in the World War 1 period in Eastern Europe, possibly the last, or one of the last, of the species. We can estimate what they look like, we can analyze their bones and fossils, but we cannot recreate them or have not yet. The woman who was possibly a Neanderthal was not DNA-tested, and thus, it is not conclusive that she was, in fact, Neanderthal. Only from her appearance and her demeanor was her Neanderthalness supported. Her characteristics match the known differences. Her size, stature, and strength were greater than normal sapiens.

It is presumed that the Neanderthal migrated from Africa to Europe hundreds of thousands of years before, long before modern man did. According to evolutionary theory, *Homo sapiens* originated in North Africa, migrated northward, developed races with differences in skin color and other features, about sixty thousand years ago, moving through the Middle East, to Europe. There evolved, at that time, as the current theory goes, many variations of the same species or what we now call races. And this is all quite clear to scientists, i.e., physical anthropologists, that there is a logical progression. Races, such as black, white, and Asian, theoretically show how different physical characteristics mutate or evolve in response to different environmental situations. Neanderthal may have evolved from Erectus before *Homo sapiens* evolved, also from Erectus.

Homo floresiensis stood 3.5 feet tall, lived until as recently as twelve thousand years ago.

Homo sapiens idaltu was a species that dates to around 160,000 years ago from Ethiopia. Cranium size was around 1460 ccm.

Denisovan was a species that is now extinct, with a 2010 finding in Siberia dating to forty-one thousand years ago, and their origin was possibly before Neanderthal. Little is known of their anatomy because all that was found were bones from a finger and a toe and two teeth. Their DNA is different from Neanderthal, but there is evidence of Denisovan crossbreeding with Neanderthal species.

Cro-Magnon was a species that is considered European, early modern human, dating from around forty-three thousand years ago, the earliest finding, and up to twenty thousand years ago for the most recent. There is evidence of crossbreeding with Neanderthal species.

A comparison of cranium size supports evolutionary theory. The cranium size for Neanderthal exceeded that of modern man. Also, the development of tool use and production, complex societies, clothing, and agriculture developed from the greater cranium size of Erectus, extending eventually to even greater cranium size of the *Homo sapiens*. The entire story of evolution during man's development from apes to our current form appears to have progressed quite logically. Size of cranium, as determined from fossils, shows a steady increase in size over several million years as humans evolved from apelike to modern human form.

There is a fairly clear representation, a steady increase in cranium size of various premodern human species, as a percentage of body mass doubling over more than 3 million years. The implication is that prehumans developed larger brains and greater intelligence over the period, eventually leading to better tool-making, social developments, and ultimately, cultural and technological developments.

Recent findings and scientific analysis indicate that there were many forms of humans, now extinct, whose time of existence overlapped, so interbreeding occurred. Yet today we see only ourselves and no clear examples of other species of Homo around on Earth. Mars may bring us a different story, if and when we get there.

However, regardless of the seemingly open-shut case for evolutionary theory, if one studies and believes the findings of Chonosuke Okamura, one might find the accepted theory, as a minimum, incomplete or contrary to Okamura's findings. How could the rockpeople have existed hundreds of millions of years before man evolved? It just flies in the face of the evidence and logic. The rockpeople images suggest one of the three following:

a) Rockpeople survived global catastrophes and never completely went extinct, with modern humans the only descendants/survivors; or

b) The human species evolved at least twice to the same or near-exact point of development, with the same behaviors; or

c) The behaviorally- and anatomically-modern humans originated around forty thousand to fifty thousand years ago, coming to Earth from another extraterrestrial source.

Of course, all three are valid explanations, and one or more of them in combination could have led to modern humans. But the implication is that something dramatic occurred, around forty-five thousand years ago, that led to the modern characteristics of language and writing, fabric clothing, social gathering, buildings, wheels and roads, and metal-using civilization as compared to hunter-gathering, non-speaking, wood, bone, shell, and rock-tooled, naked or fur-wearing apelike creatures.

Are We Evolved Primates or Alien Beings?

The main and primarily important question raised is this: If mankind, as seen in the rockpeople, lived long before the theoretical past 5 million years evolutionary cycle, from chimpanzee to *Homo sapiens*, then it raises the question of whether we truly evolved from primates as modern scientific theory goes, or did we somehow come upon the scene in an entirely different manner? Are we chimpanzees with larger brains that walk upright, speak language, and developed music, or are we aliens? It seems either is possible. Behind this question is the logical well-known progression of evolution theory versus the virtually-ignored and unexplored world of rockpeople. Thus, the common modern scientific beliefs lead to the commonly-accepted understanding that we are simply intelligent chimpanzees that wear clothes, talk, and walk.

But if we evolved from chimps, then why do the people in the rocks, millions or billions of years older than ourselves, look and act so similar to ourselves (wearing clothes, trimming and styling hair, devising tools, such as sunglasses, telescopes, houses, cars, etc.) long before chimpanzees evolved?

And if we simply are crossbreed aliens that migrated from another star system over 4 billion years ago, how is it that anthropologists-paleontologists cannot find a *Homo sapiens* fossil older than two hundred thousand years old?

Another question, which is related to and derived from the primary question, is that if aliens came to our star system, from another similar system, when ours formed, how is it that they got here? The meteorite human image examples seem to give a hint.

Size

How did some of the people in rocks (likewise, those on Mars, Moon, and other solar system bodies) get to be so gigantic, such as the examples of the Indian Head in Canada and the Greenland head-shaped land area? Similarly, how did they get tiny and microscopic as we can see in the rocks, in the *Apollo* Moon photos, and on Mars rover photos? Are we Earthlings actually growing and shrinking ourselves just so slowly that we don't even realize it? Or is Earth immune to size-change like on other bodies because of some special environmental condition, such as geomagnetic field or our relatively thick and protective atmosphere? We know there are giants and midgets in our world today, with a diverse size difference, from the smallest to the largest people. But the size of Earthlings is within a factor of ten, while elsewhere, it varies by factors of thousands. Will that change over a very long period, like a million years from now? We have legends and myths of tiny people like pixies. We see records forever falling on the smallest and largest people on Earth. We also have legends and records of giants like the Greek gods. At this time, however, we can observe that there is a much-smaller range of sizes of people on Earth today than in the mythical past. With dinosaurs, the large ones went extinct, while smaller reptiles survived. Some species of animals—turtles, lizards, crocodiles, and even monitor lizards are examples, but there are, of course, many more—survived through the 65-million-year-ago extinction event.

People Covered the Earth

The amount of rocks that contain images of people is so extensive, so vast, that it implies that the Earth was once covered with people of many sizes. Is it even possible for there to be so many people that they cover the surface of the Earth's land area? Mathematically, we know that if the number of people increases, regardless of the rate and regardless of the size of the people, and the land area never increases, then clearly, there will be a point in which the land area is covered with people, assuming that the resources support it. There may be a question of how those people can be sustained as there are known limited resources of food, energy, and water. Massive populations today die from conditions that limit water in some areas. Large people would consume large amounts of food and water, so how could they exist on the Moon where water is supposedly scarce? There are also questions of the problems that we would encounter with such a condition. Another question arises about people: We know that increased density results in increased crime rate and increased conflict between people, so doesn't it seem likely that we are approaching a limit to density of civilizations? One thing we know is that people are adaptable, and therefore, we can assume that the problems that arise can and will be dealt with in some manner due to mankind's intellect.

8

———

Conclusions

Rockpeople

Hundreds of millions of years ago, the Earth was at one or more times, not just populated, but it was also overpopulated. The land area on Earth was covered with people, plants, and animals of various sizes. Although they are observable with small effort, rockpeople today cannot be seen or believed in because of our lack of records and scientific knowledge. However, their record has been captured in rocks, and by studying their rock petrification process, we can study and learn about them.

We can see that they were like us, yet of different sizes; tiny as grains of sand and gigantic like mountains. We can see that they were of races, black, white, red, and yellow, just as we are today. We can see that they wore clothing like ours today: men with hats, shirts and pants; women with dresses; and even some animals like dogs and cats that wore sunglasses and hats. We can see that they had families and were proud of their offspring. We can see that they were technically intelligent, building devices like sunglasses, telescopes, and even automobiles. We can observe them in rocks all over the Earth and in every stone on the Earth's surface, so we know they were covering the surface of the Earth when they became frozen, and the Earth has gone through repetitive extreme flooding.

Instant Freeze

The people in the rocks were instantly frozen. We can see them standing upright with their eyes and mouths open as if they had not an instant to cringe or blink or fall down or run away. The freeze occurred so fast, people were frozen within seconds in positions that vaguely indicated the cause of the event. Some vomited as they froze, leaving a cloud near their mouths. Some vomited blood, suggesting rapid atmospheric loss. Some pointed to the horizon or looked in the sky, suggesting that they saw something ominous approaching.

The cause has to be of a magnitude equal to the effect, and the only explanation is that the Earth passed very quickly through a gaseous medium that was very cold. Jupiter has such an atmosphere, with temperatures around -320 degrees Fahrenheit. The elimination of atmosphere by itself could not cause instant freeze worldwide. Under that condition, people would fall to the ground before freezing. With no other alternatives, except possibly other gaseous planets, such as Saturn, Uranus, or Neptune, one needs to conclude that Earth passed through the atmosphere of Jupiter.

Deluge

Understanding the silification process suggests that the frozen bodies were siliconized or petrified before they thawed. When a tree petrifies, it obviously does not move during the process. But when people are petrified, it suggests that they are submerged in water, which passes through many cycles of thaw and freeze, causing the petrification without the living beings changing shape or decaying from oxidation.

Re-evolution

The various species that predated modern man, such as *Homo erectus*, Neanderthal, Denisovan, Idalta, and such early man forms, give undoubted evidence that there was an evolutionary process that occurred during the past several million years. However, since there are images preserved in rocks of much-older humankind, the process seems more appropriately thought of as "re-evolution." And 5 million years is a brief, almost instantaneous, interval when compared to the age of the Earth.

Interplanetary Exchange

There seem to have been times in the ancient past that Earth either collided with other solar system bodies or passed very close with exchanges of life-forms resulting. This is not evidenced by rockpeople so much as on Mars, where various dinosaurs suggest a regular pattern of exchange between planets. The rockpeople, having been instantly frozen, suggest an interplanetary approach, with Earth passing into a very cold medium. In fact, the cause of interplanetary collisions, as outlined in my previous books *Life on Mars*, was the sunpartners. As many as three sunpartners seem possible per extinction charts. Perhaps the people we are looking at, older than our solar system, came from one or more of those sunpartners, admittedly yet to be found.

Species

Chonosuke Okamura considered and even named the mini rockpeople and animals a different species from our own; he called them *"Homo sapiens mini"* and *"Canis mini,"* no doubt because he saw them only as tiny. He studied them only in a particular location, in limestone from nearby mountains in Japan. In fact, he wrote about them as being one size only. However, I have seen them to be of many sizes, much smaller and much bigger than the people he wrote about. It is probably not appropriate to give a separate species name to every size, for size varies infinitely. They are, in my opinion, *Homo sapiens sapiens* as they look and act just like ourselves. They seem odd to us because of our limited experience on Earth, but looking at photographs from the Moon and other planets, it is clear that they inhabit the solar system profoundly.

Life-Death Cycle

Mankind's spread over the planet appears to have happened several times over hundreds of millions, in fact billions, of years. The population of mankind

---

seems to go through a recurring cycle from near or complete extinction brought about by cosmic catastrophes to overflowing and overpopulation. The Earth appears to have been covered at one time with mankind, while at present, there seems to be relatively low numbers. We are fortunate to live in a time when the Earth is not covered with people, for there are inherent difficulties with overpopulation. We know that as density increases, problems multiply: Food, water, and space become more scarce. As technological as man can be, he cannot seem to prevent criminal behavior among portions of his population. And yet the rockpeople seem to have no such difficulties.

Apollo **Program**

The *Apollo* program, as great as it was, missed a tremendous opportunity. They walked among tiny people on the Moon, even trampled them underfoot and underwheel. But they either did not see them or refused to acknowledge their existence. At least they brought back a few rocks. But they stood, right next to them, tiny people that they could have brought back with them for scientific study. What would DNA analysis of people from the Moon show us? Is their DNA different from our own?

Continuity

The commonly-accepted theory of evolution of mankind, *Homo sapiens*, is that he evolved from chimpanzees or apelike beings with larger brain capacity, who walked upright around 5 million years ago (*Australopithecus afarensis* a.k.a. Lucy). The existing form of *Homo sapiens*, including all worldwide variations (races) is currently believed to have evolved on Earth in the approximate time span of the past three hundred thousand years. There were "anatomically-similar humans" around one hundred thousand years ago that were physically like us but behaviorally not. Speech, wearing of clothing, agriculture, communal living, writing, and technological development all occurred, according to current understanding of human evolution, within the past seventy thousand years.

In conflict with the commonly-accepted theory of evolution, the age of the stones containing images of rockpeople absolutely brings deeply into question the validity of that modern evolutionary theory. The rock images suggest that either mankind has lived continuously throughout billions of years of time or mankind evolved more than once or at least two times (once upon or before the solar system formation and again, a second time, over the past 5 million years). Mankind evolved from simple life-forms, like amoebas and worms, over a period estimated as 600 million years based on fossil observation. Alternatively, did human form survive the interplanetary calamities and catastrophes over billions of years by planet-hopping or by deep caves or some other similar occurrence? Seeing the similarity in form of the people 400 million years ago and those today, one has to presume, disregarding multiple evolutions or re-evolution, that somehow man escaped annihilation and has persisted on Earth through all cataclysms. In fact, the similarity of the human form and dress, comparing today's modern humans to those on other planets, the Moon, and in the rocks on Earth, suggests that there has been complete continuity of the human form over more than 4 billion years.

The people I am looking at, on planets, comets, asteroids, and the Moon, as well as in the geologic record on Earth, suggest that there was a time prior to known history on Earth in which the Earth was covered with people of many different sizes, from microscopic to super gigantic. There are currently such various sizes, as I pointed out in my first three books, on Mars, on other planets, and on the Moon. Could they still exist on Earth?

Why would people on Mars and Earth's Moon seem in overpopulated situation but not on Earth today? There must have been some catastrophe that killed all people on Earth but not elsewhere in prehistoric times, not just prediluvian times, but millions of years ago. We know that 65 million years ago, there was an extinction event that killed all dinosaurs. Perhaps that event also killed the humans, if there were any on the Earth at the time.

The dates of rocks seem to indicate that there were humans on Earth from its early formation billions of years ago. This is supported by the minimen in rocks throughout the Earth. Subsequent events may have caused their extinction or near extinction many times. The Earth was at times covered with people, but an event caused their near extinction millions of years ago and again and still again. The Earth was covered with people who were then mysteriously flash-frozen, petrified, and brought to near extinction. However, each time there seems to have been survivors to carry on the human venture on Earth.

———